HAUNTED
WANDSWORTH

HAUNTED
WANDSWORTH

JAMES CLARK

TEMPUS

Frontispiece: Spring-heeled Jack leaps from the shadows, terrifying Mary Stevens. (Anthony Wallis: www.ant-wallis-illustration.co.uk)

First published 2006

Tempus Publishing Limited
The Mill, Brimscombe Port,
Stroud, Gloucestershire, GL5 2QG
www.tempus-publishing.com

British Library Cataloguing in Publication Data.
A catalogue record for this book is available from the British Library.

ISBN 0 7524 4070 5

Typesetting and origination by Tempus Publishing Limited.
Printed in Great Britain.

CONTENTS

ACKNOWLEDGEMENTS

My very grateful thanks to everyone who helped me put this book together and my apologies to anyone I have overlooked here: Mary Caine, Christine Clark, William Clark, Mike Dash, Jon Day of Capall Bann Publishing, Reverend Christopher J. Davis, Ray Dickenson, Helen Evans, Roland Goodison, the late Andrew Green, Norah Green, Michael Hillman, Philip Hutchinson, Mark Justin, Thomas Kielinger OBE, Leigh from the 'Remarkable Women' website, Christopher Lomas, Darren Mann from the 'Paranormal Database' website, Craig Marcham, Pauline Martignetti, Stewart McLaughlin, Dave McMann, Joe McNally, Alan Murdie, T. Peter Park, Barbara Russell, Mike Saunders, Robert Schneck, John Smith, Stewart Smith, Chris Walton, May Whammond, Clive Whichelow, Mike White.

Special thanks must go to the following: Jayne Ayris for looking over the finished typescript and offering helpful feedback; Anthony Wallis of www.ant-wallis-illustration.co.uk for creating the illustrations used in the sections on Battersea's 'Poltergeist Girl' and Spring-heeled Jack and for his map of Wandsworth Borough; my brother Steve for endless technical support; my parents for all manner of assistance; and to the always helpful staff at Wandsworth Local History Service.

INTRODUCTION

Where might you find the most frightening thing in the world? The perhaps surprising answer is: within the London Borough of Wandsworth!

Such was the opinion of the late actor Jon Pertwee. When discussing the relative merits of setting science-fiction dramas on fantastical alien worlds or on our very own home planet, the Earth, the ex-Doctor Who star would favour the latter, explaining that there was nothing more alarming than coming home to find 'a Yeti sitting on your loo in Tooting Bec.'

His point, of course, was that there is genuine creepiness in that peculiar juxtaposition of the everyday and the extraordinary; where what should be the comfort of familiar surroundings instead only highlights the uneasy feeling that something is not quite right. Stories of uncanny experiences do not come only from the gloomy ruins of ancient castles, or the overgrown churchyards of remote country villages. Plenty of tales can be found much closer to home – from the next road perhaps, in one of the neighbouring buildings, or maybe even within your own house. This book brings together ghosts, mysteries and legends from throughout the London Borough of Wandsworth, within the boundaries drawn when local government was reorganised in 1965. It is not a huge area and probably not one that naturally springs to mind when thinking of the supernatural, yet from within these boundaries come numerous stories of homes plagued by poltergeists and encounters with ghostly figures. There is even a guest appearance from that demonic Victorian bogeyman known as Spring-heeled Jack.

The research for Haunted Wandsworth was carried out as part of 'Project Albion', which is run by ASSAP (the Association for the Scientific Study of Anomalous Phenomena). The eventual aim of this ambitious project is to record and collate mysteries and folklore from all across the country in what has been called a 'Domesday Book of the paranormal', and previous Albion titles have included Mysterious Kingston (1996), Strange Kingston (1997), Strange Mitcham (2002) and, on the internet, Strange Croydon.

While many of the stories in this book represent incidents where people have genuinely had experiences for which they could find no natural explanations, others might more readily fall into the category of ghostly legends. It will often be clear which type of story is which, but sometimes the line between legend and reality is less distinct than might be supposed, and so it will occasionally be up to the reader to decide how much to believe and how much to simply enjoy. All I can honestly state is that I have done my best to record these tales as accurately as possible. They have been gathered over a number of years, from a large variety of sources including original newspaper articles, books and, wherever it was possible, first-hand accounts from the people involved.

I hope you enjoy reading this collection of weird tales from the London Borough of Wandsworth. If you know of any other strange stories from here (or indeed anywhere else) I would be delighted to hear from you.

James Clark, 2006
writer@clarkweb.co.uk

Chapter One

BALHAM

The Curious Case of Charles Bravo

It is easy today to overlook the site of Wandsworth Borough's most infamous crime. Hidden behind the flats of Wimborne House on Balham's Bedford Hill, as if shying away from an unfamiliar modern age, are the stuccoed white walls of a nineteenth-century building named 'the Priory', a building with plenty of strange tales attached to it.

Ghosts at the Priory

My father grew up in this neighbourhood. He lived in nearby Oakmead Road and remembers the stories told by young boys around here in the years just after the Second World War. They knew the Priory as a 'haunted house' and did their very best to avoid the place, but sometimes their journeys left them no choice but to take the footpath across Tooting Bec Common, and when they reached the section of fence beyond which the old building crouched among dark trees and overgrown bushes, they would run past just as quickly as they could.

Christine Russell (who would later marry my grandfather) also lived in Oakmead Road during the late 1940s and early 1950s. She and her friend Maureen were in their teens at the time and had little interest in the scary tales told by young boys but they too knew the Priory as a place to be avoided. They had heard that a witch lived there.

During the 1950s (according to an article in the *South Western Star* of 8 October 1982), a resident of one of the flats in this building returned home from an evening out and was preparing for bed when he was disturbed by a noise from the next room. It sounded remarkably like schoolboys having a pillow fight but when he went to check the room it proved to be quite empty. Perhaps, however, the pillow fight really did take place, albeit many years earlier, because around the end of the nineteenth and beginning of the twentieth centuries, the Priory was home to Harlington boys' school.

More recently, writer James Ruddick visited the Priory whilst working on a book about a death – a probable murder – here in 1876. Although it was beyond the scope of Ruddick's own

The Priory, Bedford Hill. (James Clark)

Tooting Bec Common: footpath running beside The Priory. (James Clark)

research interests, he had previously heard that the building was supposed to be haunted by the ghost of the murder victim, one Charles Bravo. The story he heard involved a woman who slept in Bravo's old room one night and awoke a little before dawn to find the room deathly cold and the apparition of a man standing at the foot of her bed, gazing down at her. When her host later showed her a photograph of Charles Bravo, she identified that man as her ghostly visitor. Only then did her host admit that other people had reported strange feelings and noises in that room, even objects being moved. During Ruddick's own visit towards the end of the 1990s, he spoke to one of the Priory's residents, a young man whose girlfriend claimed to have seen and heard this ghost so often that they eventually called in a priest to perform an exorcism. That had been three weeks before Ruddick's visit and it had, he was told, put an end to the haunting.

Other Priory residents are highly sceptical of the idea that the building is or ever has been haunted, and despite living here have never experienced anything untoward themselves. Indeed, there are two very good reasons for believing that the ghost stories here spring ultimately from the depths of human imagination.

The first is the building's striking appearance. Looking like something out of a children's storybook, the Priory's gleaming white exterior is a fantastic example of early nineteenth-century Gothic, complete with turrets and imitation battlements. That alone might be enough to inspire colourful tales about the place.

The second reason is that, quite apart from any ghosts that may haunt the place, the Priory is already shrouded in mystery and has been for well over a century. In fact, 'The Balham Mystery', as it was dubbed at the time, is one of the most famous unsolved cases in the annals of British crime. It is well worth looking at this case in some detail, not only because it is fascinating in its own right but also because the events are key elements underlying the ghost stories in the two sections that follow: 'The Ghost in the Garden, page 17 and 'Strange Happenings at the Bedford,' page 19.

The Death of Charles Bravo: A Victorian Murder Mystery

Charles Bravo was a barrister in his early thirties who lived at the Priory with his wife, Florence. On Tuesday 18 April 1876, he returned home badly shaken from a riding accident. That night he retired to his room shortly before ten o'clock, where he changed into his nightshirt, brushed his teeth and then, as he did every night, took a drink from the water jug he kept on his bedside table. After rubbing a little laudanum onto his gums to soothe his toothache, and swallowing a small amount more to ensure a sound night's sleep, he climbed into bed.

A short while later, the door to his room flew open and Charles rushed out onto the landing shouting for someone to bring him hot water. Then he stumbled back inside, reeling with dizziness and doubled over with violent stomach cramps. After vomiting out of the window, he collapsed.

Despite the subsequent efforts of half a dozen doctors, including the famous Sir William Gull (physician to Queen Victoria and suspected by some of being Jack the Ripper!), Charles spent the next few days in agony before finally dying early on Friday morning. A post-mortem confirmed the cause of death to have been poison: a massive dose of tartar emetic, a derivative of antimony. But what had happened? Was it suicide or murder? And if murder, who killed Charles Bravo?

Some believe Charles committed suicide, that he deliberately swallowed poison but then panicked and cried out for help. This suspicion was first raised by his peculiar reaction when told he had been poisoned. He did not demand an investigation, nor did he appear overly concerned as to who had poisoned him. As the *Daily News* of 12 August 1876 put it: 'The curious demeanour of the dying man – who was not indifferent to life, but utterly indifferent to the cause of his own death – unsuspecting, casual – was so strange it defies conjecture.'

Sir William Gull himself believed it was suicide, stating: 'It would be surprising to me if I were to tell a man that he was dying of poison, and he was not surprised; it would induce me almost to think he knew it.' Further support for the suicide theory comes from the statement given to the police by Florence Bravo's live-in companion, Mrs Jane Cox. She said that before Charles died he confessed to her that he had swallowed poison.

But why would Charles kill himself? His zest for life was well known and none of his friends who had met him in the days and weeks before his death believed for one moment that he had been contemplating suicide. Even the man in charge of the case – Detective Chief Inspector George Clarke – recorded that he found 'no motive whatever for Mr Bravo to have taken his own life'. To his doctors, Charles strenuously denied taking any poison and, as will be seen later, there is reason to disbelieve Mrs Cox's account of his supposed confession. As for Charles's curious indifference to his plight, one suggested possibility is that he was suffering a side effect of the poison, which can affect the body's central nervous system and cause confusion.

The majority of those who have studied the case agree that Charles Bravo did not kill himself but was murdered, yet from that point onwards opinions diverge. There is endless argument as to who the murderer was, and the colourful cast of suspects appear so perfectly fitting for a murder mystery that they could have stepped straight from the pages of an Agatha Christie novel.

Mrs Florence Bravo

First, there is Florence, Charles's young and alluring wife. Petite and pretty, with blue eyes and lustrous auburn hair, she seems to have been an exceptionally strong-willed woman, especially for Victorian Britain. She persuaded her first husband, Captain Alexander Ricardo of the Grenadier Guards, to leave the army for her, but this decision was to have tragic consequences. Finding civilian life too boring, the military man turned to brandy and womanising, and when he eventually became physically violent towards Florence, she walked out on him.

Florence sought refuge at her parents' home but the prospect of her leaving Alexander appalled them so much that they threatened to disown her unless she returned to him. They persuaded her to take a restful break at the Hydro, a high-class sanatorium in Malvern, Worcestershire, where they hoped she would come to her senses. Unfortunately for this plan, there she met Doctor James Gully and Gully agreed to help her separate from her husband.

Before Florence and Gully could act, Alexander died of haematemesis, brought on by his alcoholism. His demise was possibly hastened by the same type of poison that would later kill Charles Bravo and various students of the case believe that Alexander was Florence's first victim. Some Victorian wives occasionally slipped into their husband's drink just enough antimony to cause nausea: a form of aversion therapy to curb excessive alcohol consumption. This might explain the severe bouts of vomiting the hard-drinking Alexander had suffered shortly before the couple separated.

Upon Alexander's death, Florence inherited approximately £40,000, a fortune for that time, and with her newfound freedom she decided to move closer to London. She was soon joined by a very close companion: Dr Gully. Florence and Gully had fallen in love during her visit to the Hydro and they had begun an affair, even though she was still married to Alexander at the time and Gully, although estranged from his wife, was also married. To make matters worse, Gully was in his mid-sixties, almost forty years older than Florence. (The scandal that would result

Leigham Court Road, Streatham. (James Clark)

from the affair's eventual discovery was one reason people were so ready to suspect Florence of murder a few years later.)

Florence took a villa in Leigham Court Road in Streatham and Gully moved into another villa in the same road, almost opposite hers. The lovers were reasonably successful in concealing their affair until one afternoon when they were caught in a most compromising position on the drawing room sofa of Florence's solicitor. Little spreads so swiftly as gossip and Florence quickly found herself a social outcast, shunned by her peers. A period of serious illness followed, brought on by a miscarriage (or possibly an abortion), and although Florence's companion, Mrs Cox, slowly nursed her back to health, her love affair with Gully did not survive.

Florence and Gully appear to have remained close friends however, for when she moved to the Priory in the leafy and fashionable suburb of Balham in March 1874, the doctor followed, taking a house just a few minutes' walk away, which he named Orwell Lodge. But if Gully still harboured any hopes of winning back his young lover he was to be disappointed because just a few months later Florence met Charles Bravo.

It was Mrs Cox who masterminded their meeting. She knew better than anyone just how lonely Florence had become and realised that the only way Florence could regain respectability was by finding the right husband. Florence and Charles were duly married in December 1875 at All Saints church in Kensington, but the happy day was by no means the end of Florence's troubles.

From the very start, the marriage was probably due more to mutual convenience than to love. Florence desperately wanted to be accepted back into society, and Charles's motives were just as mercenary: he wanted Florence's money.

Unsurprisingly, the arrangement soon began to fall apart. 'I cannot contemplate a marriage,' Charles once stated, 'that does not make me master in my own house' and although such a situation was quite normal in the 1870s, it was not one the strong-willed Florence was prepared to accept. The atmosphere grew increasingly strained as the couple struggled for power until, just a few weeks after the wedding, Florence fled once again to her parents' home. Soon, though, the fear of finding herself socially ostracised for a second time drove her back to the Priory.

Florence was trapped. She could not leave Charles because it would ruin her forever and he would never leave her because that would mean abandoning her money. Also, Charles was determined to have a son and heir but when Florence did fall pregnant she miscarried and sank into depression. Desperately ill, she took to her bed knowing that as soon as she was fit enough, Charles would insist upon trying again for a child. Genuinely scared for her health, and perhaps even her life, did Florence despairingly decide that her only way out was to murder her husband? Getting access to the poison would have posed little difficulty: as a keen horsewoman, Florence would have known about the tartar emetic often kept in the Priory's stables to worm the horses. And remember the suspicions over her first husband's demise…

Florence left her sick bed on Easter Monday, 1876. The following evening, Charles Bravo was poisoned. Before moving on to consider the other chief suspects, it is worth briefly considering the theory that Charles's death was not murder at all but an unfortunate accident. According to this version of events, Florence did administer poison but only intended to incapacitate Charles so that he would be too ill to make love to her that night; unfortunately, her heavy drinking earlier that evening led her to misjudge the dose she slipped into his water jug. It is possible that some Victorian women did use antimony in this manner, as a drastic form of contraception, but many historians are sceptical about this. In any case, it is difficult to consider the amount of antimony that found its way into Charles's water jug as a slight overestimation since it was at least three or four times the lethal dose.

It seems more likely that Charles Bravo was murdered. Florence has always been a favourite suspect and it is true that she seems to have had both the motive and the means to kill her husband, yet attention has been drawn to one very compelling reason to believe her innocent. There is little doubt that the poison was in the water jug, but about four hours after Charles took his fatal drink one of the doctors attending him – Dr Johnson – drank at least one full glass of water from the same jug and was unharmed. The poisoned water must have been replaced at some point with fresh water, presumably by the murderer so as to delay identification of the poison and thus any possible treatment for Charles. But between the time Charles drank the poison and the moment Dr Johnson drank from the same jug, Florence was never once on her own. She could not have refilled the water jug without somebody noticing.

But if Florence didn't kill Charles Bravo, who did?

Doctor James Gully

The second suspect is Dr James Manby Gully, a celebrated physician of the day whose patients included such famous names as Charles Dickens, Florence Nightingale and Charles Darwin, as well as prime ministers William Gladstone and Benjamin Disraeli. A short, balding man in his sixties he nevertheless possessed enormous personal charisma, enough to cause the much younger Florence to fall in love with him when she visited his sanatorium in Malvern.

Gully had the means to commit murder. As a doctor he would have had little difficulty getting hold of the poison that killed Charles Bravo, and he also seems to have had a motive. His affair with Florence cost him dearly. He left Malvern to follow her, first to Streatham and then to

Balham, and the discovery of their affair ruined his professional reputation. After everything he sacrificed for her, he must have been devastated when Florence ultimately rejected him and chose to marry Charles instead.

Another reason for suspecting Gully is the series of anonymous letters delivered to Charles at the Priory shortly after his wedding. Described by Charles as 'vile', the letters claimed he had married Florence only for her money and Charles was quite convinced they came from Gully and that the doctor hated him with a passion. Among those commentators who believe Gully was the murderer was the crime novelist Agatha Christie. Writing in *The Sunday Times Magazine* of 20 October 1968, she stated: 'I've always felt [Gully] was the only person who had an overwhelming motive and who was the right type: exceedingly competent, successful, and always considered above suspicion.'

Yet those who knew Gully personally thought of him as one of nature's true philanthropists. He donated to the poor, set up medical charities and generally dedicated himself to saving lives, not taking them. If Gully had had a motive it would have been his furious resentment towards Charles for stealing Florence from him, but the evidence actually suggests that Gully had come to terms with Florence's decision. After their affair ended, Florence met with Gully in secret when she was worried that Charles was only after her money. According to Florence's account of this meeting, the doctor listened to her fears, gave her sound advice as to what financial arrangements she should make and encouraged her to marry Charles for the sake of her future happiness. This accords with later testimony by Gully's butler, who gave evidence that when he and the doctor watched Florence's wedding procession pass by Orwell Lodge, Gully 'expressed the hope that she would be happy'.

Although opinion was set firmly against him before the inquests, both jury members and the general public became convinced that Dr James Gully was an innocent man.

George Griffiths

Suspect number three is George Griffiths, the Bravos' coachman until Charles sacked him towards the end of 1875. Ostensibly, he was dismissed because of a recent accident – he was driving Florence and Mrs Cox when he collided with a wine cart in Bond Street – but it is likely that Charles simply wanted an excuse to save money.

It was a terrible blow for the recently married Griffiths, who was losing not only his job but also his home, since the cottage he shared with his pregnant wife was part of the Priory's estate. He was given two weeks' notice to leave.

Griffiths was furious and his bitterness led to an interesting incident. On the Bravos' wedding day, Griffiths was drinking in the bar of the Bedford Hotel, at the bottom of Bedford Hill. Sullenly nursing his mug of porter, he turned to the manager and announced that Charles Bravo would 'get what was coming to him'. He would, said Griffiths, be dead within four months. It was a curiously prophetic statement, which must have seemed even more suspicious when the later police investigation found that Griffiths had made several purchases of tartar emetic.

There is no doubt that Griffiths bore great resentment towards Charles but was he a murderer? Admittedly, it does seem likely that it was Griffiths, and not Gully, who penned the anonymous letters sent to Charles, because the timing is too coincidental otherwise: the first letter arrived soon after Griffiths was given notice and the letters stopped when he moved away. But regarding the murder itself Griffiths had a strong alibi. A decent coachman was always in demand and he quickly found new employment with Lady Prescott in Herne Bay in Kent. Lady Prescott herself vouched that Griffiths had been working for her at the time of the poisoning. As for the tartar emetic, there was really nothing suspicious about a coachman purchasing this as the substance was widely used as a horse medicine. As Griffiths put it at the inquest: 'Antimony is good for worms and the "black bots" in horses.'

As for the 'threat' made at the Bedford Hotel, Griffiths claimed this actually referred to an incident that had taken place shortly before, in which Charles was bitten by a dog. All he had meant, he said, was that he thought Charles was going to die of hydrophobia as a consequence of the bite.

This excuse sounds unlikely but, having weighed up all the evidence, Detective Chief Inspector Clarke was satisfied that Griffiths was no murderer.

Mrs Jane Cox

The last of the four suspects is Mrs Jane Cox, Florence's live-in companion. She was a small woman of around fifty years old, who invariably dressed soberly and whose long black hair was combed back into a tight bun above her pinched and sallow face. The two women made an unlikely-looking pair – the one beautiful and richly attired, the other quiet and wrapped in dark clothing – yet they had become close friends.

Mrs Cox has always been a popular suspect, and not only because of her somewhat sinister appearance. To begin with, there is the fact that she told the doctors and police that she rushed to help Charles the moment she heard his cries, yet according to the maid, Mary Ann Keeber, those cries went unanswered until Mary Ann herself went into Florence's bedroom to fetch help, where she found Florence lying drunk on the bed and Mrs Cox sitting on a stool, knitting. Another problem with Mrs Cox's version of events is her claim that Charles admitted taking poison. The maid was present in the room when Charles is supposed to have said this, and she denied that any such confession took place.

Then there is the impression one gets that Mrs Cox deliberately hindered the doctors' attempts to treat Charles. Rather than send straightaway for Dr Moore – the Bravos' family doctor who lived nearby in Balham – Mrs Cox sent for a doctor who lived several miles away, in Streatham. Then, when the doctors wanted to examine a sample of Charles's vomit to find out what he had swallowed, they learned that Mrs Cox had cleaned out his sick bowl. And they might have been quicker to diagnose an irritant poison if they had realised he was bleeding internally, but Mrs Cox had already removed his bloodstained nightshirt and had it placed into the laundry.

Most damning of all, Mrs Cox seems to have had a strong financial motive. She had numerous debts hanging over her, a mortgage, and three sons to bring up on her own, her husband having died some years earlier. Living at the Priory with her meals provided, she had no living costs and was able to pay off her mortgage by letting out her own home. But Charles, who felt threatened by the strong bond between Mrs Cox and Florence, had been claiming that she was too expensive to keep on now that Florence had a husband to take care of her, and he was keen to dismiss the live-in companion.

Her impending financial catastrophe has convinced many that Mrs Jane Cox had sufficient reason to commit murder, but writer James Ruddick has cast doubt on this theory. Mrs Cox's relative, Margaret Cox, the owner of three plantations in Jamaica, had been seriously ill for some time and being childless had decided to leave everything to Jane and her three sons. At the time of the murder, Mrs Cox already knew that she was due to inherit a sizeable fortune, as indeed she eventually did. When Margaret died in 1879, Jane Cox's inheritance totalled some £6,800. Knowing this, is it really feasible that she would risk not only her own life but also the future security of her children by slipping poison into Charles Bravo's drinking jug?

'The most mysterious poisoning case ever'

These, then, are the suspects: Mrs Florence Bravo, Dr James Gully, George Griffiths and Mrs Jane Cox. Each might have had his or her own reasons for wishing Charles Bravo dead yet there are compelling reasons to believe each of them innocent of murder. Someone was responsible for Charles Bravo's death, but who?

Inquests into the death were held at the Bedford Hotel. (See 'Strange Happenings at the Bedford', page 19, for the ghost stories associated with that building.) As the scandalous details of Florence's romantic relationships were publicly and sensationally dissected in the newspapers, huge crowds were drawn to Balham, all eager to learn the latest details. At last, the jury returned its verdict: 'We find that Mr Charles Delauney Turner Bravo did not commit suicide; that he did not meet his death by misadventure; that he was wilfully murdered by the administration of tartar emetic; but there is not sufficient evidence to fix the guilt upon any person or persons.'

So Charles Bravo was officially a murder victim but the precise details of what happened remained an enigma. For well over a century now, that enigma has proved irresistible to countless people, each seduced by the intricate puzzle of overlapping motives and alibis in this real-life whodunit.

The writer Henry Keating has described the Bravo affair as 'the most mysterious poisoning case ever'. Another writer, Jonathan Goodman, has called it 'one of the greatest mysteries in modern crime', while to a third writer, William Roughead, the case is 'the prize puzzle of British jurisprudence'. Yet despite the decades of study and the thousands of pages written about this case, no final consensus has ever been reached.

The mystery of what happened at the Priory on the night of 18 April 1876 remains unsolved.

The Ghost in the Garden

Not all the odd stories connected with the Bravo Mystery are confined within the Priory's castellated white walls. The next section, 'Strange Happenings at the Bedford', discusses an alleged haunting at the Bedford public house, site of the inquest into Charles Bravo's mysterious death, but first another tale from Bedford Hill, close to the Priory itself.

This incident was reported in the *South Western Star* of 13 August 1982. The article does not make it clear exactly when this took place although it would appear to have happened some months, or more likely years, earlier.

Mrs Barker was a retired schoolteacher and, according to John Bradbury who interviewed her, was not at all the sort of person you would suspect of making up a story just for effect. Originally from Baslow, near Chatsworth in Derbyshire, she had since moved to Tooting Bec where she lived in Elmbourne Road. Her great passion in life was gardening and when one day she noticed the plants growing beside a recently demolished house, she asked for and was granted permission to explore the garden and salvage whatever flora she wished. The article states that this garden and what remained of the house stood 'adjacent to the Priory' on Bedford Hill.

And so, on a bright and oppressively hot summer's afternoon, Mrs Barker visited the garden to see what she could find. With her were her daughter – Mrs Diana Brandenburg – and Sheba, Diana's experienced Alsatian guard dog. As Mrs Barker quietly examined a shrub of the genus Artemisia, her pleasant reverie was interrupted by a scream from Diana. Mrs Barker hurried across to her daughter and it was immediately obvious she was badly frightened. With a shaky voice, Diana said she had seen what the article described as 'a motionless pall of dirty smoke

Bedford Hill: the Priory is hidden just behind the large building on the right. (James Clark)

stationed over a withered rose bush', and whatever it was had obviously spooked Sheba because the normally brave guard dog had fled in terror across Tooting Bec Common, later to be found by the railway embankment there. And, eerily, despite the summer heat there was a very noticeable icy chill in the immediate vicinity of the bush.

Despite her daughter's unnerving experience, Mrs Barker returned to the garden several days later. Thankfully there was no sign of the strange dark smoke but while she was examining the plants Mrs Barker happened to glance towards the Priory and spotted a pale young lady dressed in a blue cloak. This lady was standing in the shadow of a tree, yet any thoughts that she was just a neighbour enjoying a peaceful afternoon in the garden vanished when a startled Mrs Barker realised that the tree's trunk was clearly visible through the young lady's body.

The retired teacher must have been made of stern stuff indeed for, rather than beat a hasty retreat in the face of the unknown, she instead moved in closer to examine the apparition. As she did so, stated the article, she was able to see 'an aura of light running parallel with the contours of the body; not a halo, but something like a thin glowing wire that reminded her of a magnesium flare.' For some reason, Mrs Barker became utterly convinced that to actually touch the apparition would prove fatal and so she held back a short distance and just observed. Abruptly, the apparition was gone and Mrs Barker found herself alone in the garden once again.

The evening after her encounter, Mrs Barker made a sketch of the spectral lady, and she later turned this into an oil painting. If any reader knows the present whereabouts of this painting, I would be very interested to hear from you.

The railway embankment on Tooting Bec Common. (James Clark)

In 1982, Mrs Barker was finally able to put a name to the apparition when she came across a photograph in an old copy of *Picture Post*. Although she had at the time been unaware of the mysterious death at the Priory in 1876 it seems that Mrs Barker may somehow have glimpsed an after-image of those tragic events for the photograph – unmistakeably of the same figure she had seen beneath the tree – bore the lady's name. It was Mrs Florence Bravo, wife of the allegedly murdered Charles Bravo.

Strange Happenings at the Bedford

The Bedford public house, at No. 77 Bedford Hill in Balham, deserves its fame as one of the best pubs in London. It is well known as a venue for live music and comedy, and has won multiple awards including the prestigious *Evening Standard* 'Pub of the Year' prize in 2002. It is strange, then, to recall that this lively building once housed the grim inquest into the still unsolved death of Charles Bravo.

Given the connection with that enduring mystery it comes as little surprise to learn that the Bedford has itself been called haunted. There have been reports of a ghostly grey figure being glimpsed here and at least one dramatic event was blamed on supernatural forces. Talking to the *Balham & Tooting News* (7 December 1973), then-manager Lee Harris stated: 'About two years ago, the piano fell off the stage for no apparent reason. The incident happened at about midnight,

The Bedford public house, Balham. (James Clark)

after a group had been playing jazz that evening. Nobody pushed the piano. We think it must have been the ghost. Possibly he didn't like the music.'

This article suggested that the ghost was that of Charles Bravo himself, haunting the scene of the inquest into his death and forever angry at the decision reached. A little more than a year earlier, however, a different newspaper suggested that the ghost was actually that of Dr James Gully, one-time lover of Charles's wife and a suspect in his alleged murder. This article, in the *Evening Standard* of 24 August 1972, quoted an earlier manager, Michael Guest, as saying that he had not been at the Bedford long but 'everyone' claimed there was a ghost in the building. Guest also mentioned the piano incident and that some people held the ghost responsible.

The main emphasis of this *Evening Standard* article, however, was on a Spiritualist's attempt to solve the Bravo mystery once and for all by getting in contact with the phantom haunting the Bedford. Working on the assumption that the ghost was that of Dr Gully, Mrs Sandra Oland sat alone in the room where the inquest had been held, playing tapes of classical music to try to attract his spirit. Sadly, her efforts did not result in the breakthrough she was hoping for.

The temptation to link the reported haunting here with the Bravo mystery is indeed great, but this connection may not be appropriate. When Lee Harris spoke to the *Balham & Tooting News*, he gave a brief but clear description of the ghost, which he claimed to have seen himself. He described it as a 'shimmering grey' figure and said that it had been seen 'quite often in the ballroom, which was once the billiards room'. Although this was the very room where the inquest was held – supporting the contention that the ghost was that of either Bravo or Gully – Harris was also adamant that the ghost 'was a man wearing Tudor-type clothes and aged between sixty-five and seventy'.

A Tudor phantom hardly seems in keeping with a Victorian murder and so, if the Bedford really is, or was, haunted, it would seem that the true underlying story remains to be discovered.

Chapter Two

BATTERSEA

Battersea's 'Poltergeist Girl'

Half a century ago, Battersea was the setting for one of the strangest poltergeist cases ever recorded. The events began in a Victorian terraced house at No. 63 Wycliffe Road, home at that time to the Hitchings family whose teenage daughter Shirley was about to become famous as the 'Poltergeist Girl of Battersea'.

At the end of January 1956, Mr Walter Hitchings, a London Transport motorman, discovered a key lying on fifteen-year-old Shirley's bed. None of the family recognised this key, nor could they suggest where it had come from, but with the benefit of hindsight its mysterious arrival signalled the appearance of a poltergeist that would plague their lives for the next few years. As Shirley walked into the house on 4 February, there was an odd creaking noise and soon afterwards 'strange thumps and raps' began to sound occasionally from walls and from under Shirley's bed, sometimes becoming so loud that the next-door neighbours complained. Beginning on around 9 February, small household objects including an alarm clock, a pair of scissors and various china ornaments started to move about of their own accord. Very quickly, it became apparent that the antics of the poltergeist – jokingly referred to by the family as 'Charlie Boy' and 'Spooky Willie' – were centred on Shirley. When she was home, her parents told one reporter, 'clocks fall from mantelpieces, table lamps are levitated [and] objects disappear and turn up in the next room'.

During the week ending 17 February 1956, the Reverend W.E. Douthwaite, vicar of St Bartholomew's, called at the house hoping to be able to get to the bottom of the mystery but despite his best efforts he could find no explanation for the strange events and left as baffled as everyone else. On Saturday 18 February, Shirley accidentally dropped a glove on the floor and when she bent down to retrieve it, it flew up into the air and hit her father in the face. Later that same night, Mr Hitchings and Shirley's older brother, John, who was in his mid-twenties, stayed up to keep watch after Shirley went to bed. Mr Hitchings later gave an account of what happened:

> First we heard tappings from her bed. They went on for a long time. Then Shirley said the
> bedclothes were being pulled under her so we got hold of them and felt that they were being

Wycliffe Road, Battersea: only the northern end survives today. (James Clark)

tugged by force. While this was going on we saw that Shirley was being lifted out of her bed. She was rigid and about six inches above the bed when we lifted her out and stood her on the floor.

Following this apparent levitation, Shirley seemed unharmed and was able to describe the sensation, saying: 'I could feel a force pushing into the centre of my back and lifting me up.' In an attempt to escape the poltergeist's attentions, Shirley spent a night at a neighbour's house, but the taps and knocks followed her there. According to the neighbour, Mrs Lily Love who lived at No. 61, 'She spent a night with us but none of us got any sleep because of the noise. We were all scared.' The poltergeist also demonstrated that it could follow Shirley further afield. Sometimes when she travelled on a bus, other passengers would hear the rapping sounds, and the problem even followed her to the West End store where she worked as a cutter in the dress department. When some of her colleagues became badly frightened by the inexplicable thumps heard in her vicinity her bosses told her to stay away from work until the noises stopped.

Inevitably, reports came to the attention of local journalists and the *South Western Star* sent reporter Ross Werge to investigate. When Werge arrived on Monday 20 February he interviewed the whole family, including Shirley's grandmother, Ethel Hitchings, an elderly lady in her mid-seventies who lived on the first floor and who was at first reluctant to confirm that anything unusual was going on. In fact, she informed Werge that the story was 'a lot of rot'. But as he continued to question her, Grandma Hitchings admitted having seen slippers fly through the air and finding clothes pegs mysteriously unpegged just seconds after she had secured them herself. On one occasion, she said, she was mixing a pudding when a spoon suddenly jumped into the bowl. Werge dutifully reported the background as given to him by the family but the main focus of his article was a remarkable interview he was able to conduct, a three-hour 'conversation' with the poltergeist itself.

Shirley had already told Werge that Spooky Willie was able to use the knocks and thumps to communicate with her and so at around half past two that afternoon a hard wooden chair was provided, on which Shirley placed her foot and Werge his hand. Soon, a faint but distinct 'irregular thump' began, which seemed to emanate 'from the wood itself'. Despite watching Shirley's foot intently the reporter was sure she was not deliberately producing the sounds herself. At one point, he asked her to move her foot to the outside edge of the chair to see what effect that might have but it made no difference. Furthermore, the sounds also came while Shirley was leaning against a wall, or against a cupboard on the other side of the room.

Using a simple and well-known code – one knock for 'No', two for 'Yes' and three for 'Don't know' – Werge proceeded to ask the poltergeist a series of questions:

Are you evil? – No

Can we help you in any way? – Yes

Have you a message for Shirley? – Yes

Will you deliver it today? – No

Tomorrow? – No

On Sunday? – Yes

(If the poltergeist ever really intended to deliver its message on Sunday, its plans were presumably interrupted by an attempt that day to exorcise it: see below.)

When asked how old Shirley was, the poltergeist answered correctly with fifteen 'distinct thumps' but it appeared rather uncertain as to its own identity. At first, it claimed to be Grandma Hitchings's mother who had died forty years previously, but later it claimed to be 'a boy named Donald, who used to play with Shirley'. (A slightly different account of this latter version was recorded by another contemporary investigator of this case, H.S.W. Chibbett, whose lengthy article appeared in the US edition of *Fate* Magazine in October 1959. According to Chibbett, the poltergeist was 'an "entity" who claimed to have lost his life by drowning in the English Channel' and who 'became known to the family as "Donald", because he said he resembled a near neighbour of the Hitchings who had gone abroad.') In any case, the names Spooky Willie and Charlie Boy fell into disuse and people began referring to the poltergeist as Donald, the name by which it is best remembered today.

Before visiting the Hitchings's home, Werge had by his own description been extremely sceptical about the story but by the time he left he claimed to be no longer quite as certain. The report he wrote for the *South Western Star* appeared on 24 February 1956 and concluded: 'Perhaps there is a natural explanation, but it has me beat. And I take a lot of convincing.'

Exorcising Donald

Wednesday 22 February 1956 saw the first attempt to exorcise the poltergeist. Harry Hanks, fifty-two, a London Underground train driver and friend of Mr Hitchings, was a non-professional medium and he invited Shirley to his home in Groveway, Stockwell, to take part in a séance. Things did not go smoothly. By this time, the poltergeist was a national news story and Hanks, a committed Spiritualist who had seen an opportunity to publicise the Spiritualist movement, allowed numerous reporters, photographers and TV cameramen to cram themselves into his sitting room, which already held another half dozen people making up the circle of sitters. (Footage of the séance was later aired on television but unknown to viewers the images shown were not genuine, having been staged for the cameras after the real séance was over. Hanks refused to allow filming during the actual event.)

Despite the media scrum the séance got underway, but before long proceedings were interrupted by a hammering at the front door. For once, the poltergeist was blameless: it was the police, who had received a report of a black magic ceremony being conducted on the premises! Hanks was furious, complaining the interruption had 'broken down the aura' and the incident led to questions being asked in Parliament, when Lt-Col. Lipton, Labour MP for Brixton protested that Hanks deserved an official apology. In reply, the Home Secretary, Major Lloyd-George, defended the police's actions, explaining that they were responding to information received and only carrying out their duty. The police remained on the premises for around a quarter of an hour but once they ascertained the true circumstances they left without taking further action and the séance resumed.

'The police broke down conditions temporarily,' said Hanks afterwards, 'but they were built up again later and I completely removed the poltergeist from the child.' At first, it seemed he was correct, that Shirley was indeed free of Donald. The following day, however, the appalling behaviour of two men claiming to be journalists upset whatever delicate balance the séance had created. They called at the Hitchings' home at around noon, persuaded Shirley's parents to let them take her to a doctor to be examined, and drove the teenage girl first to an office in Fleet Street and then out through the West End to a private house in an expensive area somewhere in the suburbs. 'The rooms had very thick doors,' Shirley remembered afterwards. 'They took me into a room and offered me a liqueur. I refused.'

A psychiatrist entered the room and for the whole of the remainder of that afternoon he attempted to hypnotise the frightened teenager, who did not really understand what was going on. Rather than obey the psychiatrist when asked to relax and watch the pen moving in front of her eyes or stare into a glass ball, Shirley constantly fidgeted, patted her face to keep herself alert, walked around and pleaded to be allowed home. At last, the psychiatrist gave up and Shirley was taken back to Wycliffe Road to arrive home some six hours after she had left. At about eight o'clock that evening, the poltergeist disturbances started up again.

As before they began with rapping noises. These grew gradually louder and louder and at around twenty past eleven, a photograph in a glass frame flew from the mantelpiece and hit Shirley's mother in the back. The following morning Mr Hitchings telephoned Hanks to ask for help, and within half an hour the part-time medium was walking through their front door. When Shirley told him what had happened the day before, he decided the events had utterly demolished the protective aura he had established, meaning that the séance would need repeating from the beginning, only this time without a pack of reporters present. He took Shirley with him in his car and she spent the rest of that day (Friday) and all of Saturday and Sunday at the Hanks home, where Hanks, his wife and his daughter Dorothy prayed for her and ensured that nobody else was allowed near.

On the evening of Sunday 26 February, a second séance was held at the medium's home. Present were the three members of the Hanks family, Shirley's father, two experienced mediums named Daisy Bennett and Ada Roden, W.F. Neech (a reporter for *The Two Worlds* Spiritualist newspaper and the only reporter allowed to attend), two young friends of Neech's who had won Shirley's confidence, and of course Shirley herself. Before the séance began, according to Neech's report of 3 March 1956, 'the temperature in the room dropped suddenly' and 'icy breezes seemed to race over the hands of the sitters' but there were no dramatic interruptions this time and the séance was seemingly successful. For the second time in a few days Hanks announced that Shirley's troubles with Donald were over.

He did warn, however, that the cure might not be permanent. Hanks believed that the psychiatrist's interference on Thursday had broken down his own previous work, and that this was why the poltergeist returned that evening. Shirley, he said, was a natural medium whose undeveloped psychic powers had attracted an earthbound entity to her. He claimed that this entity was the spirit of a woman who had lived in Wycliffe Road some years ago and committed suicide. Hanks had 'rescued' this particular spirit, he said, but could offer no guarantee that trouble would not flare up again. It was a prophetic statement.

When Shirley awoke one morning in early March, she found her wristwatch crushed on the table beside her, and soon after this episode the knocking sounds returned. By now, Shirley's father had adopted a simple method of taking down messages from the knocks using an alphabetic code: one knock for 'A', two for 'B', and so on, and the poltergeist, it seems, was only too eager to communicate. 'Sometimes he insists on talking to us until dawn,' Mrs Hitchings said. 'If we take no notice, he starts throwing things at us.' Grandma Hitchings had seen a milk bottle fly past her head and Mr Hitchings had been forced to duck to avoid a framed picture of himself that leapt off the mantelpiece. The constant strain on the family was becoming difficult to take. Both Grandma and Mrs Hitchings were being treated for nerves and Mr Hitching's doctor had ordered him a fortnight's sick leave.

Fire!

On the night of Sunday 11 March, the poltergeist warned that the house would be set on fire unless Shirley contacted a particular journalist who had written a sceptical article about the paranormal. (The journalist was not named in the newspaper report of this incident, an article in the *South Western Star* of 16 March 1956.) The poltergeist's message concluded with the words: 'Okay, it is your master.' Not long after this message was received, Shirley and her mother were preparing for bed when they saw two flashes of light in quick succession, which they described as 'like short circuits' and which so unnerved them that they slept in the living room rather than the bedroom that night. Some time later (the timing is not clear in the report), Grandma Hitchings saw a lighted match float over Shirley's head and fall to the floor at her feet.

Late on Monday morning, Shirley cried out to her father that she could smell burning and when Mr Hitchings ran into the downstairs bedroom he found the sheets and eiderdown alight. He managed to beat out the flames with his hands but had to go to the hospital afterwards to be treated for burns. Detectives who later called at the house declared they were unable to find the cause of the fire.

A few days later, the poltergeist seemed to grant Shirley leave to take a short break at her aunt's house, rapping out the following message: 'DON'T THINK ABOUT ME / TAKE THE GIRL [T]O NELL / IF I TAP I ONLY PRAYING / FOR YOU GO WITH NELL / LITTLE ONE THINK OF GOD / GO IN PEACE.' That night, Shirley did visit her aunt's house, where she enjoyed a rare peaceful night, but the next day she was taken back to No. 63 Wycliffe Road in a police car after there was a series of 'violent disturbances' in her aunt's house.

During the week between Saturday 17 March and Friday 23 March, a reporter for *Psychic News* named Christopher Riche-Evans made several visits to the Hitchings home. In his subsequent article (24 March 1956) he offered his first-hand opinions of the family, describing Shirley's parents as 'a sincere, pleasant couple' who were 'genuinely anxious to rid themselves of the nuisance which has been interfering with their sleep, and affecting their health for the past nine weeks', and Shirley herself as 'a likeable, attractive young girl, gifted with imagination and a sparkling personality.' Although he experienced nothing strange personally during his visits, he made a comprehensive list of events that had happened to that date; in addition to those phenomena already described, Riche-Evans recorded that the house had often been permeated by a strong scent of violets, which would be followed by a decidedly less pleasant stench, sometimes similar to burning rubber and at other times like a sewer. There had also been mysterious draughts, sudden drops in temperature, strange whistling and hissing noises and, on one occasion, 'a kind of whirlwind in the room.'

By the end of March, there had also been claims of a whispering sound being heard (attributed to the poltergeist's 'voice') and another attempt had been made to get rid of Donald. A healer named Mrs W.M. Durrant, accompanied by a control medium, spent an evening at the house but, although she reported making contact with a 'presence', her efforts did nothing to bring the phenomena to an end. A few weeks later, newspapers were reporting further attempts at arson.

On Sunday 29 April the electric cooker apparently switched itself on, setting fire to some rags on top of the stove. An hour later, Mrs Hitchings had to quickly snatch away a sheet that had been placed onto an open coal fire. Further fires broke out the following day, beginning at two o'clock in the afternoon and continuing sporadically until a quarter to nine that evening. Two neighbours, Charles and Doris Baker from No. 67, helped to fight the blazes but by nine o'clock the exhausted Mrs Hitchings could take no more and she dialled 999. Police and fire investigators were yet again dispatched to the house, where they were shown the charred remains of tablecloths, brushes, towels and items of clothing and asked to believe that a poltergeist was to blame. Understandably, they preferred to point the finger of suspicion at Shirley and she was questioned for almost an hour. The teenager denied the charges and her parents continued to stand by her: 'Everyone thinks we are crazy,' said Mrs Hitchings, 'and that Shirley does these things. It's nonsense.'

This seems to have been the last of the arson attempts, although two reporters from the *Daily Express*, unaccompanied by any of the Hitchings family, later tried to communicate with Donald by using an upturned wine glass in the manner of a ouija-board planchette and claimed to receive a message hinting at further attacks to come: 'Fire me do. Me do it again.'

The situation had become so threatening that Grandma Hitchings had fled the house to stay with relatives. There are no reasons to suspect that Donald followed the old woman, but it does seem that two other people were trailed by the poltergeist after leaving the Hitchings home. The first was a friend of Mr Hitchings who is unnamed in the newspaper report but described as an 'Underground Railway motorman' and so was probably Harry Hanks; he was 'astonished to hear thuds coming from under his feet when he hopped on a bus after a recent visit'. The second man, also unnamed, was an insurance agent who later 'heard strange knockings in his home'.

Andrew Green Investigates

Of all the many people who became involved with this story, the investigator who became most associated with the case was paranormal researcher Andrew Green, who was initially asked to look into the story by the *News Chronicle*. By the time of his death in 2004, Green had authored seventeen books and hundreds of articles on ghosts and hauntings, and the Shirley Hitchings case is mentioned in many of his writings, notably in his classic *Our Haunted Kingdom* (1973).

Green described Shirley as a 'typical agent' of poltergeist phenomena, noting that she was rather 'highly strung'. He also recorded that she was anaemic, an only child and that her private life seemed to revolve around just two interests: a deep fascination with French history and the morbid worship of the young film star James Dean, who had been killed in a car crash a few months earlier in September 1955. Green's first visit to No. 63 Wycliffe Road took place before Grandma Hitchings left to stay with relatives and it did not take long for him to be convinced that something genuinely strange was going on. In a letter to me dated November 2003, he stated:

Following my interview with Shirley and her father (her mother, who had obviously suffered from a severe burn on her right arm, was obviously too sedated to provide any real information) and her grandmother (who was too engrossed with TV to notice or acknowledge my existence), I requested 'Donald' (the 'poltergeist') to walk downstairs – he had been in the upstairs bedroom whilst we chatted in the front sitting room. I was, as you can imagine, surprised on hearing footsteps descending the stairway and stopping outside the open doorway of the sitting room where we could see that the hallway was empty.

After extensive interviews with Shirley and both of her parents, it was apparent to Green that the family's day-to-day life now revolved around Donald to a substantial degree. They had come to accept 'his' reality thoroughly, so much so that they were reluctant to leave the house, even to go to work, without first obtaining the poltergeist's approval. Mrs Hitchings was particularly wary of going out to do any shopping without 'his' permission because the poltergeist often 'put things into the shopping bag that I hadn't purchased'.

Other poltergeist pranks reported to Green included the throwing of ink onto a ceiling and the front bedroom's decoration with the covers of a weekly film magazine stuck to a wall with jelly. Green also personally experienced the mysterious knocks that had so impressed Werge. He heard these frequently, as did two trainee journalists that the *News Chronicle* assigned to follow the case with him. He noted that the knocks were not random but could be produced on demand in response to specific questions, and he also observed that Shirley would squeeze her eyes shut for a few moments before the sound was produced, as if she were summoning up the power needed to create the effect. Although he initially believed that the teenage girl might be making the sounds herself by 'cracking her joints' he soon concluded that this was not the case because the knocks did not always emanate from Shirley herself. Rather, they might originate several feet away from her, from the wardrobe on the other side of the bedroom, for example, or from the ceiling.

The Poltergeist Turns French

So far, the poltergeist had already been given or had claimed a number of different identities: Charlie Boy, Spooky Willie, the mother of Grandma Hitchings, a boy named Donald, and/or a woman who committed suicide. In May 1956, during a conversation via an upturned wine glass, the poltergeist started to claim yet another identity, now stating that 'he' was the spirit of Louis Capet who, according to the poltergeist/Shirley, had been born on 16 July 1798 and was the illegitimate son of King Charles II of France. 'Louis' apparently chose to contact Shirley because she resembled a Portuguese princess he had once known! (In retrospect, the first hint of this French identity had come at the end of March when the words 'Dauphin' and 'Dolphin' appeared in communications, together with a reference to 'lost in the Channel.')

The Hitchings family treated this new story with great scepticism, as did Green who was surprised by Shirley's insistence that she very rarely read books and had no knowledge of French history; it was impossible to square these claims with evidence from the narrow bookcase beside Shirley's bed, which held around thirty books, of which more than half were about French history. Moreover, the details she gave regarding Louis were incorrect; as Green told me:

> Shirley was wrong in stating that the son of Charles II of France was the alleged entity, known as Louis Capet, born in 1798, 'who fell in love with her as she resembled a Portuguese princess, when he was alive'. She had got the completely wrong date for such a character, but she was highly imaginative and spraying hysteria around which affected both the trainee journalists that had been allocated the 'assignment' [...] Both admitted that they had not even noticed the wealth of books in Shirley's bedroom devoted to James Dean and French history. Much was also mentioned by her of Duval 'the well known Highwayman', who had also contacted her (but we never gained any reason for this).

Someone else who investigated and wrote about the case during this period was H.S.W. Chibbett, described by Green as 'a Spiritualist', whose previously mentioned *Fate* article records many details about the poltergeist's claims to be Louis. According to Chibbett, the Louis in question was the second son of Louis XVI and Marie Antoinette of France, who had been born in 1785. On the death of his elder brother in 1789, this Louis became Dauphin, or heir to the French throne, and after his father was guillotined during the French Revolution, exiled French noblemen proclaimed Louis to be the new king of France: Louis XVII. His final years were spent in prison where, despite rumours of his escape, it seems he died in 1795.

Chibbett notes that an early hint of this new personality came in a message on 15 April 1956, three weeks before the claim to be Louis: 'I come to tell what I look like – five foot high, fair head, blue eyes, 35 wide'. Later, Louis gave details of his attire: 'Satin, a tail coat, knee breeches, hose, lace waistcoat, black buckle shoes.'

Week after week, the messages continued to come as Louis communicated a mass of information about his life in France in the late eighteenth century. Sometimes the messages contained words in French (not always correctly spelled) and much of the historical data seemed impressively accurate, although Shirley's own interest in French history should be remembered.

The French theme was continued in drawings that began to appear on walls and ceilings throughout the house, and which Shirley firmly denied making herself. Many were of fleurs-de-lis, with the words 'Roi Louis' written beneath, while others were of crossed swords superimposed over shields. They first appeared on the walls of the sitting room and it was in this room that the poltergeist seemed to feel most at home. In accordance with 'his' wishes, Shirley kept a number of dolls in here, dressing them as per the poltergeist's instructions, as the following message received on 2 June 1956 illustrates:

> Let us give that doll a French Royal formal name . . . Oui . . . let us think . . . let it be Marie Antoinette, mon de mere name. She must be her for she has a French face. Let me put the flurdeley on her, because my mother had it branded. Will you dress Marie as I describe: she must have six petticoats, two skirts, a top – you know, her hair all curls, a fan, shoes, the top square neck, long sleeves with lace edges – lots of lace – silk too.

On one occasion, after examining a fleur-de-lis design on the shoulder of the Marie Antoinette doll, Chibbett asked out loud if the poltergeist would demonstrate how it made these marks. A few minutes later, with Shirley, her father and her mother all in Chibbett's full view, Mrs Hitchings exclaimed: 'What's that on your arm, Shirley?' On the upper part of Shirley's bare left arm was a small fleur-de-lis, looking as if it had been drawn or stamped there using dark-blue indelible ink, and after another few minutes Chibbett noticed a similar mark on the right side of Shirley's neck.

Although 'Donald' now claimed to be 'Louis', many of the poltergeist's antics remained essentially the same as before. The night of 10 June seems to have been particularly busy in this regard and Chibbett records a number of phenomena said to have taken place. That evening, Shirley could not find some of her clothes and these were later discovered inside the piano, where they had been pushed down past the strings. Later, as Shirley and her parents were together in the dining room, a knife flew out from the kitchen area and embedded itself into the dining room window frame. After the family went to bed (they were all sharing the same bedroom at this time), their bedclothes were interfered with and 'violent' scratching sounds were heard, as well as 'rappings as though on metal'.

That same night, Shirley cried out that there was something 'furry' at the foot of her bed, and this turned out to be a bundle of red flock roughly six inches (fifteen centimetres) in diameter. Investigation revealed several slits in the quilt, through which the flock interior had been extracted. Shirley refused to get back into the bed after this, spending the rest of the night in a wicker chair.

Worse, as if the earlier incident with the flying knife was not worrying enough, further violence was reported. A pair of scissors was flung towards Mr Hitchings and later, as Shirley was getting dressed in the morning, a screwdriver was thrown at Mrs Hitchings as she lay in bed, catching her a glancing blow on the back. In the kitchen, a kettle of boiling water was overturned twice, the second time almost scalding Shirley's feet.

Letters from a Poltergeist

But if the poltergeist that came to Battersea in 1956 is famous for any one thing in particular, it is for the remarkable series of letters it allegedly wrote. The first suggestion of written communication came in the last week of March, when a number of scribbles, only occasionally legible, started turning up on pieces of paper. A few months later, on 27 June, Chibbett was told that Louis had left a sealed envelope for him. Walking into the sitting room, he found that a number of the dolls dressed by Shirley according to the poltergeist's instructions were posed on the settee, with 'Marie Antoinette' arranged as if sitting on a throne and the others – including 'Anne Boleyn' and 'Lady Jane Grey' – curtseying towards her. Shirley told Chibbett that Louis had placed the dolls in these positions 'himself'. On the coffee table was an envelope, and inside this Chibbett discovered a local newspaper, on page nine of which was a message written in ink. At first this appeared to be nothing but a scribble but when Chibbett realised the lettering was reversed he was able to read it using a mirror. It read: 'Out in one month. Don't worry, Shirley.' (Interestingly, the original message contained the same spelling mistake in the word 'month' that was often made by Donald, indicating that 'Louis' and 'Donald' were at some level the same.) Unfortunately, the promise to depart in a month's time was not honoured; instead, the poltergeist seemed to become keener than ever to communicate with people.

On 13 August Louis gave a message for Mr Hitching: 'I want a pen that you put black water in and it writes. Not a quill pen. I want one like Shirley has got. I can keep my own diary like I did.' The poltergeist was duly provided with a notebook and a fountain pen, after which writing was occasionally found on the notebook's pages. These early attempts at written communication were barely decipherable scrawls but later, as if Louis were gradually becoming more skilled at writing, several people started to receive letters that had apparently been written and sent through the Royal Mail by a poltergeist.

Probably the first to arrive was that received by Chibbett on the morning of 1 November 1956. This was the forerunner of 'an ocean of mailed correspondence' and Chibbett records that he was continuing to receive letters at the time of writing his 1959 article. Among the other recipients were a number of dignitaries, including Lord Brabazon, and Andrew Green who received three letters and a Christmas card.

Chibbett declared himself unsure as to the true source of these letters, asking: 'Am I the recipient, through Her Majesty's Mail, of letters from a poltergeist, from a clever Shirley Hitchings, or from His Royal Highness, Prince Louis Charles Philippe, Duc de Bourbon?' Green, on the other hand, was in no doubt that Shirley had penned the letters herself, despite her denials. Not only did the teenage girl seem noticeably apprehensive when he asked her how an invisible poltergeist might purchase the necessary stamps and writing materials, but also the 'poorly-disguised handwriting in appalling French and English' was clearly her own. Moreover, although Green deliberately avoided mentioning the letters to Shirley, she spontaneously asked him whether the poltergeist had contacted him, suggesting that she was well aware of their existence.

By November 1956, Shirley had been sacked from her job at the West End store and had lost another job as a civil servant after claiming the poltergeist pulled her off the bus as she travelled in on her first day. The poltergeist itself was reportedly displaying new abilities and could now make ghostly moaning sounds and mew like a cat. It also allegedly told the Hitchings family to leave No. 63 Wycliffe Road, although they presumably ignored the warning. If they thought that the affair was almost over they were to be disappointed because the poltergeist was to remain an unwelcome houseguest for a long time still to come.

The Poltergeist and the Missing Children

One interesting incident rarely mentioned in discussions of this case is Louis's attempt to solve the tragic 'Babes in the Wood' mystery, which occurred in June 1957, more than a year after the poltergeist's first appearance. On Thursday 20 June of that year, seven-year-old June Sheasby and her five-year-old brother Royston disappeared near their Bristol home. They were last seen by a group of older schoolchildren as they walked hand in hand along the bank of the weed-choked River Frome, making their way towards a place where stepping stones would enable them to cross the river to the side where their home lay. A massive hunt for the children in which the police were aided by around a thousand members of the public failed to turn up any clues and when the story was picked up by national newspapers it aroused countrywide sympathy.

Back in Battersea and communicating via an upturned wine glass, Louis declared that he knew where the Sheasby children could be found, prompting the female journalists accompanying Andrew Green to insist that they immediately take Shirley up to Bristol to help in the search. Mr Hitchings approved and Green agreed to accompany the trio as far as the railway station. The following account of what happened next was given to me by Andrew Green:

> Whilst sitting by myself in the bus, but in the row in front of where Shirley was sitting (the reporters were at the far, front end of the bus) I turned and asked if [the poltergeist] was still with us, to which I received the usual response of seeing her screw up her eyes and hearing

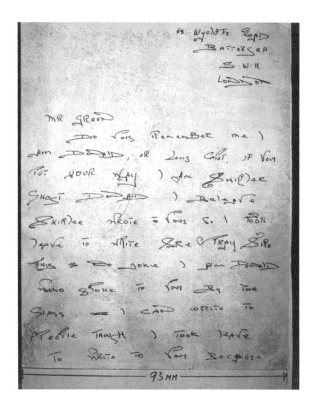

Letter sent to Andrew Green, allegedly written by the poltergeist. (Norah Green)

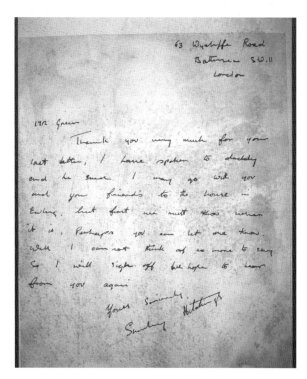

Letter sent to Andrew Green, written by Shirley Hitchings in a similar style to that supposedly written by the poltergeist. (Norah Green)

a 'thump' beside her, whilst being a little surprised to see the seat sink down as if someone (invisible) had sat next to her. [The poltergeist] had already demonstrated his 'skill' by knocking on the pavement of the street as we walked along Wandsworth High Road...On arrival at the main line station (I fear have forgotten which), and whilst waiting for the next train, the three had a cup of tea in the canteen and were surprised to see the spoon in Shirley's cup rise out of the cup and fly across the room much to the confusion of a couple of other customers.

The two journalists and Shirley arrived in Bristol on the evening of Friday 27 June and somehow persuaded the police to shift the focus of their search away from the river and onto a disused reservoir near Portbury. Owned by the Bristol Waterworks Co. and known locally as 'The Pond', this reservoir measured approximately sixty feet (eighteen metres) by forty feet (twelve metres) and was eight feet (two-and-a-half metres) deep. A team of four divers carefully searched its murky waters but found nothing and after two hours the search was abandoned.

Despite the tip-off's unusual source and despite the waste of police time, the *Bristol Evening Post* for Saturday 29 June reported this event in a surprisingly matter-of-fact way, stating simply: 'The woman who gave the police the original information arrived in the city last night and said she was in contact with the spirit, a 17th [sic] century prince. "His" messages led her to the pond.'

Louis later apologised for 'getting muddled' and offered to take the reporters to the correct location but this offer was ignored. The bodies of the two missing children were discovered on the evening of Monday 1 July. They had been buried in a shallow grave in thick undergrowth in the grounds of Snuff Mills Park, in an area known locally as 'The Grove', some miles from the location given by the poltergeist. Nobody was ever charged with their murder.

Conclusions

Green records that the poltergeist, which first manifested in the early months of 1956, lasted into 1958, gradually decreasing in intensity as Shirley matured (although the Hitchings's next-door neighbours continued to complain of knocking sounds waking them in the early hours of the morning). Chibbett's account has the poltergeist lingering even longer, noting that reports of activity were still coming from the house as late as May 1959. It is clear, then, that compared with a 'typical' poltergeist disturbance, which might fade away after just a few weeks or months, Battersea's Wycliffe Road episode lasted a considerable time. This is a characteristic shared with another poltergeist case that occurred in nearby Eland Road in 1927–28. (See 'The "Mystery House" of Eland Road', page 33.)

As with so many poltergeist reports, however, it is extraordinarily difficult to come to any clear conclusion as to what really happened. Were paranormal forces at work in the Hitchings household? Were the mysterious happenings truly caused by one or more discarnate spirits? Was the young Shirley responsible for a prolonged hoax? Or does the answer lie elsewhere?

Regarding the claims to be Louis Capet, Green firmly believed that Shirley herself was behind these. The teenage girl's deep interest in French history, the availability of relevant historical material on her bookshelf and the similarity between her handwriting and that of 'Louis' left him in no doubt that Shirley was the source of these messages, although he did concede that she might have been in a semi-trance state at the time and thus not consciously attempting to deceive anyone.

Chibbett, too, was somewhat suspicious about the poltergeist's claims to be 'Louis' but he was more inclined to believe that something paranormal was involved here. He felt that the personality revealed in the Louis messages was more in keeping with the identity of the French prince than with Shirley's own identity. He was also impressed by the amount of historical information conveyed by the poltergeist about life during the French Revolution especially as, according to Chibbett, Shirley did not belong to a library, had not studied French history at school and owned no books about French history. As has already been pointed out, however, Shirley did in fact possess many books on precisely this subject. Moreover, even Chibbett had to admit that although much of the historical information was accurate the authentic facts were 'interspersed with much irrelevant material and a predilection for modern affairs which line up with Shirley Hitching's own character.'

Yet, despite deep suspicions around the issue of 'Louis Capet' and the origin of the letters, most if not all of the investigators were impressed by some of the apparently psychokinetic phenomena in this case, and in particular by the knocking sounds that came from walls, ceilings and various items of furniture in response to questions. Even Andrew Green, who became convinced that much of the case was the result of hysteria and perhaps even fraud, for the rest of his life remained puzzled as to how these effects could have been produced, finally telling me: 'I can only suggest that the real cause was that of [genuine] poltergeist phenomena resulting from [Shirley's] mental state combined with the distress of living in undesirable conditions.'

Nowadays, Wycliffe Road is a very different place. Much of the road was demolished when the area was developed during the early 1970s and today, No. 63 – home of the Hitchings family and their unexpected and mysterious houseguest – no longer exists.

The 'Mystery House' of Eland Road

Poltergeist cases are not common and so it is exceedingly curious that Battersea has seen two occur just a few roads from each other. As noted earlier, Shirley Hitchings and her family were pestered by a poltergeist in Wycliffe Road during the 1950s. Three decades earlier, attention had been focused on a house in nearby Eland Road where the bizarre events taking place led the press to dub this property 'The Mystery House'.

Looking at it today, it is a perfectly normal two-storied terraced house in a pleasant suburban street lying just off Lavender Hill. In the late 1920s, it was home to the Robinson family, who had been living there for some twenty-five peaceful years when, on Tuesday 29 November 1927, a selection of small objects (pennies, pieces of soda and lumps of coal) crashed onto the conservatory roof at the back of the house. A few days later more objects fell. Thinking somebody was throwing them over the garden wall, Frederick Robinson contacted the police and when a constable arrived the two of them stood watch in the back garden. As they waited, more coal and pennies landed on the roof, yet the men were unable to work out where they were coming from. One lump of coal knocked against the constable's helmet and the policeman ran to look over the garden wall but there was no sign of any culprit.

By now, events were unsettling the family, six of whom lived together in the house. In addition to Fred (a twenty-seven-year-old tutor) were his invalid father Henry, aged eighty-six, and Henry's three daughters: Miss Lillah Robinson and Miss Kate Robinson (both schoolteachers), and Mrs George Perkins, who was a widow. The youngest resident was Mrs Perkins's fourteen-year-old son, Peter.

In mid-December, the family's terrified washerwoman declared that she was no longer prepared to work there after discovering a pile of red-hot cinders in the outhouse. There was no fire nearby and no apparent way in which the cinders could have got there.

The 'Mystery House' of Eland Road.
(James Clark)

Once again, Fred got in touch with the police and this time he and a constable waited in the kitchen to see what would happen. As they kept watch, two potatoes were flung inside! The phenomena continued to escalate and at around nine o'clock one morning a series of terrifyingly loud bangs shook the house, continuing for around one hour. Unable to take any more, Fred dashed into the street to fetch help and one of those who came to his aid was a gentleman by the name of Mr Bradbury. Bradbury later gave his own statement of events, recording that as he, a fishmonger and a greengrocer gathered in the Robinsons' home, he noticed that the women in the house 'appeared to be very frightened'.

During that morning's disturbances something had smashed the window in Henry Robinson's room and the elderly invalid was now too scared to remain in the house. With Bradbury's assistance, Fred carried the old man from his room, past a heavy chest of drawers that had been overturned by some invisible force. One of Fred's sisters (although Bradbury's statement does not say which) now decided that she was also too scared to stay any longer. Bradbury and Fred had to accompany her to her room while she packed a bag because she was too afraid to be left on her own. Afterwards, the men returned to the back bedroom where Fred showed Bradbury and the others the objects scattered across the conservatory roof, but as they were looking there was a heavy crash from another bedroom, provoking a scream from one of the women downstairs. The men raced into the bedroom to find that a chest of drawers had fallen to the floor.

As Fred and the constable kept watch, two potatoes were flung into the kitchen! (Anthony Wallis: www.ant-wallis-illustration.co.uk)

Enter Harry Price

Shortly before Christmas 1927, word of the strange events in Eland Road reached Harry Price, the famous paranormal investigator who is best remembered for his research into Borley Rectory, often referred to as 'the most haunted house in England'. In 1927, Price was working at the National Laboratory of Psychical Research in Queensberry Place, London, the research organisation he set up in 1925 to conduct experiments into the claims of mediums and psychics.

At first, Price paid no particular attention to these reports because, as he wrote later in *Poltergeist Over England*, they 'differed little from many others that I receive'. But by the early weeks of January 1928, sensational stories about this case were appearing in the press. His interest piqued (or perhaps scenting an opportunity to publicise his researches) Price decided to visit Eland Road for himself.

On the morning of Thursday 19 January 1928, Price met the Robinsons for the first time. His initial impression of the family was 'distinctly favourable'; that is, he felt it unlikely that they were perpetrating a hoax. Promising to contact them again shortly Price returned to the National Laboratory, only to find a message awaiting him from the editor of the London *Evening News* asking if Price would visit the house accompanied by a representative from that newspaper. So that afternoon, Price returned to the Robinsons' home, accompanied by a Mr Grice.

Together, they interviewed Fred to gather details of what had taken place up until that date. Afterwards they toured the house to assess the damage caused over the preceding weeks. They saw that several windows had been broken, some of which had small holes in the glass as if stones had been fired through at high speed. A glass panel on one of the interior doors was broken too, as well as a few panes of glass on the conservatory roof. The roof itself was strewn with pennies, pebbles, lumps of coal, potatoes, pieces of soda and sundry other small items.

Visiting the back bedroom, which was littered with the remains of smashed ornaments, they saw that the door panels had been 'shattered' and that a heavy chest of drawers was 'splintered as if from a fall'. Further damaged items lay in the hall, including a hat stand that had been snapped in two, two broken doors, a damaged tea tray and several fallen pictures.

Stepping outside, where more lumps of coal, soda and so forth lay scattered across the small garden, Fred pointed out two windows of neighbouring houses that had also been damaged. As Price and Grice were getting ready to leave, the poltergeist apparently decided to perform for them. They were standing in the kitchen chatting to Fred and Kate, who were the only other people present that afternoon, when something hard and solid thudded to the ground in the passage behind them. Lying on the passage floor was a large gas lighter that Kate told them was always kept on the gas stove in the scullery. It seemed impossible that somebody could have thrown the lighter there because that passage connected the kitchen to the scullery, which led directly to the garden through the door they had just closed. Nevertheless, they rushed into the garden to look for a possible culprit. There was nobody there.

Casting around for a non-paranormal explanation, Price wondered whether the Robinsons could have staged the incident by balancing the two-ounce lighter on top of the open door that led from the kitchen to the passage, and letting it fall from there. He experimented with this door and found that it would have taken a considerable push to dislodge the heavy lighter in this way, although he concluded that it was just about possible for the lighter to have been balanced carefully enough for this trick to work.

The following morning (Friday 20 January), Price and Grice paid another visit to the house. Nothing remarkable happened during the hour they stayed, although they were told that more small objects had been thrown since the previous day and yet another window had been smashed. At around one o'clock that afternoon, the editor of the *Evening News* telephoned Price at the National Laboratory with some dramatic information. The authorities had taken Fred away against his will and were detaining him at St John's Hospital in Battersea. Apparently, the police had decided that Fred was responsible for the strange goings-on at the house and so they were holding him for observation as to his mental health. In an article published in *The Two Worlds* on 14 March 1941, Fred bitterly recalled what happened:

> I was arrested by the police, outside the ivy covered house in which I had long resided, charged under the Lunacy Act, and detained in a mental ward for ten days. I had related to the police some happenings which had taken place only a few moments before. They laughed, called me mad, and took me away to be observed.

Despite Fred's enforced absence from the house, bizarre events continued to take place. The back page of Saturday's *Evening News* carried an article titled 'Mystery House: New Antics After Man Was Taken to Hospital', which reported that only an hour after Fred was taken away there was 'a series of extraordinary disturbances' in the kitchen, in the presence of Fred's three sisters. According to this article, 'a cup appeared to fly across the room, and a heavy bench from the scullery fell into the kitchen.'

Fred was detained at St John's Hospital, since converted to apartments. (James Clark)

By now, crowds had been gathering outside the house for some days. In his 1941 article, Fred told how 'Thousands of people had crowded nightly round our house' and referred to the 'hostile crowd jeering outside … the sneers of the policemen … the innuendos of Fleet Street…' Fred's resentful account was possibly a little exaggerated but it is clear that the publicity surrounding the case was causing a problem. According to the *Evening News* of Friday 20 January 1928, mounted police had to be called in to disperse the curious crowds. Price's account of the case also recorded that mounted police were needed to keep back the 'gaping mob which all day and night stood in the road and gazed, open-mouthed, at nothing more thrilling than a couple of broken panes of glass.' On the Saturday evening, some members of that mob even threatened to break into the house unless they were allowed to investigate the phenomena for themselves.

That weekend, Fred remained under observation at the hospital but his enforced absence from the house did nothing to ease the situation there. If anything, the phenomena were becoming more pronounced. In addition to the by-now familiar arrival of pieces of coal, soda, etc., an attaché case had fallen from a kitchen chair, an umbrella had sprung from the stand in the hall to the kitchen floor, a cruet had crashed to the ground, and the table had fallen over after being prepared for dinner. Chairs seemed to be particularly affected. Mrs Perkins reported that some had 'marched down the hall single file' and that she had attempted three times to lay the table for dinner on Saturday but on each occasion the chairs had stacked themselves on top of the table.

At times, the phenomena were so overwhelming that those family members who remained were forced to take refuge outside their own home. Fourteen-year-old Peter, in particular, became so terrified that he was sent away to the countryside to recover.

On the afternoon of Monday 23 January, Price returned to the house, accompanied once again by Mr Grice from the *Evening News*. After hearing about the weekend's events from the two remaining occupants (Mrs Perkins and one of the Misses Robinson) and taking another look around the building, the four of them were standing in the kitchen chatting when they heard a heavy object fall to the floor behind them. The two men immediately began to look for the fallen object and Price soon spotted something beneath a chair in the corner. Bending down to feel underneath the chair, he discovered a pair of lady's black shoes. In the right shoe, he found a small bronze ornament, apparently one of a pair of cherubs that had been on the front sitting room mantelpiece for the previous twenty-five years. When they checked, the women seemed astonished to discover that one of the cherubs was indeed missing from its usual place. Price recorded that he had been within a few inches of both women and had not noticed either of them move suspiciously. Mr Grice was also unable to understand how either could have been responsible.

Price and Grice searched the house again but found no one hiding in any of the rooms. With the sisters' agreement they decided that they would spend the whole of the following night at the house to keep watch. The sisters would doubtless have welcomed the investigators' presence overnight because quite apart from the ongoing poltergeist antics there were still problems with the crowds outside. As Price made to leave on Monday evening, he was 'accosted' by 'a burly ruffian with a Russian accent [who] asked if he could "mind the place" for me.' Price declined his services.

Unfortunately, the plan to spend another night in the house on Tuesday had to be abandoned. With most of their family now absent, the remaining two sisters found themselves no longer able to bear either the strange goings-on indoors or the overbearing crowds outside. They left, shutting up the house behind them. Despite this temporary setback to the investigation, Price returned on Wednesday afternoon. This time he was accompanied by a medium known as 'Miss X' (whose presence was the idea of the *Daily Express* news editor) and by an *Express* representative named Mr Salusbury. The trio met up with Mrs Perkins and arrived at the house at around three o'clock that afternoon.

Price took Miss X on a tour of the building to see if the medium could receive any psychic impressions. The house felt generally 'miserable' to her, she said, but the kitchen in particular caused her to feel 'chilly'. Although there was a good fire burning in the kitchen and both Price and Salusbury felt noticeably warmer in here, Miss X continued to shiver with cold. She and Mrs Perkins chose to remain in the kitchen while the two men left to search the upstairs rooms, taking care to shut the kitchen door behind them.

Just as they reached the top floor, Salusbury thought that he heard something fall in one of the downstairs rooms. They made their way back down the stairs to search the lower rooms but everything appeared to be in its correct place. Opening the kitchen door, they asked if Mrs Perkins and Miss X had heard anything. They had not.

Once more, Price and Salusbury closed the kitchen door and climbed the stairs. As they searched the front upper room they again heard an object fall somewhere in the house, and when they investigated this time they immediately spotted a piece of yellow soap lying in the passageway in clear view. How it had got there left the two men completely bemused as they had just walked along this narrow and well-lit passage six or seven times. They agreed that it would have been utterly impossible for them to pass the soap so many times without noticing it or treading on it.

Hurrying downstairs to the kitchen, they found the door still closed. Inside, the women admitted having heard something fall but insisted that they had both remained inside the kitchen the entire time. It seemed impossible that any human agency had been responsible; anyone entering or leaving the house would have to have either used the front door, which was locked from the inside, or passed through the kitchen, in full view of the women who were adamant they had seen no one.

With this curious incident, the strange phenomena in the 'Mystery House' seemed to die away as bizarrely and as pointlessly as they had arrived and, as Price observed, 'another "Poltergeist case" ended in a very unsatisfactory and inconclusive manner.' A few days later, Fred was allowed to return home, the doctors having been unable to find anything wrong with him. The elderly Henry sadly died in the infirmary, and, unsurprisingly, the Robinsons chose to move out of Eland Road.

The End?

But perhaps Price was overly hasty in concluding his investigations. According to Fred's personal recollections of the case, the poltergeist continued to persecute the family for some time after this, smashing their furniture and tearing items of clothing to shreds. In his 1941 article, Fred stated: 'Three times we were forced to move house [...] Each move, however, saw the phenomena decline in strength and now it has ceased.'

Fred's article also told of a particularly bizarre series of incidents that had apparently escaped Price's attentions, and that Fred described as 'the most wonderful piece of psychic phenomena anyone could observe'. He now claimed that during the main events of 1927–28, he had been in contact with some sort of entity that communicated with him using small slips of white paper that appeared from nowhere to drop onto the floor. Held up to the light, the paper revealed writing made, it seemed, from tiny pinholes. One message read: 'I am having a bad time here, I cannot rest, I was born during the reign of William the Conqueror.' This was among messages signed by 'Tom Blood', and other messages were signed 'Jessie Blood', supposedly Tom's sister.

It is difficult to understand how Price could have overlooked such a remarkable phenomenon, for surely someone would have mentioned it during one of his many interviews with the family members. More cynical readers may wonder if the passage of years had led Fred Robinson to (perhaps unconsciously) embroider his story. Then again, the messages were perhaps no more fantastic than an invisible force flinging lumps of coal and soda through the air.

Theories

Originally, Price suspected that the lumps of coal and other objects were being catapulted at the Robinsons' house from a particular nearby building. About eighty yards (seventy-three metres) away and clearly visible from the Robinsons' back garden were the rear windows of a private asylum housing victims of shellshock. 'The angle at which portions of the house were struck originated this theory in my mind,' he wrote, noting that there 'had also been "friction" between the Robinsons and the inmates of the mental home.' However, he discounted this theory when he learned that other incidents were taking place within the house.

Price was quite sure that no adult members of the household were guilty of perpetrating a hoax. He was also convinced of the innocence of fourteen-year-old Peter, and cited four reasons for believing this. In the first place, he wrote, Peter had been absent when many of the phenomena occurred. Second, he did not believe Peter was physically strong enough to have caused some of the damage inflicted on the furniture. Third, Price was certain that, with so many potential witnesses in the house, there was no way Peter could have played so many tricks without being caught even once. His final reason was that Peter had appeared to him to be genuinely scared by what was happening.

It has often been noted how many poltergeist cases seem to centre around an adolescent boy or girl and so it is tempting to consider Peter in this way, as an unwitting focus for paranormal events. Yet this does not seem to have been the case here since, as Price pointed out, Peter was absent during many of the strange events.

In the end, the case baffled Price who was never entirely certain that the few phenomena he personally experienced were genuinely paranormal (whatever that means!). 'The incidents of the gas-lighter, the cherub and the soap are still puzzling me,' he wrote. 'On the three occasions when I witnessed the movements of the objects I could never be quite certain that a normal explanation could not be found for the supposed phenomena.'

His eventual conclusion (of sorts) was that the disturbances were probably started by some of the soldiers in the private asylum and that the worry and anxiety thus caused provoked a reaction among the Robinsons: 'Whether this reaction was a normal or extranormal one is, in the absence of further evidence, a matter for speculation. But I consider that the evidence for the abnormality of the occurrences is much stronger than that for the theory that the Robinson family were wholly responsible for the trouble.'

Whatever the causes of the strange events of 1927–8, there is no longer any need for curious crowds to gather outside the house in Eland Road. The present occupants are thankfully untroubled by incidents of the sort that beset the Robinsons. Perhaps the final words here should be those of Frederick Robinson: 'Others may be sceptical and hurl their criticisms, but these experiences have convinced me that there are phenomena which defy material explanations.'

The Haunting of Battersea Dogs and Cats Home

If there is any truth in the widespread belief that animals – and especially dogs – are highly sensitive to the supernatural, then the one place no phantom should go undetected is Battersea Dogs and Cats Home. The home was founded in 1860 by Mrs Mary Tealby as the Temporary Home for Lost and Starving Dogs. Originally in Holloway, north London, it moved to its present site in Battersea Park Road in 1871. In the many years it has been here the home has grown so much that its buildings are today squeezed in between the gas works and Battersea's iconic disused power station. Every year, the home rescues and cares for thousands of lost and abandoned cats and dogs and it is a never-ending task: during the 1990s it was receiving around ten thousand dogs every year.

One of the kennels blocks here is named Tealby in honour of the home's founder and it is said that this is haunted by the ghost of Mary Tealby herself, whose spirit visits at night to greet newly arrived dogs. Such a tale would not be totally unexpected as there is something deeply comforting in the idea of this caring woman continuing to watch over the institute she brought into being, but there is good reason to consider this more than just another legend. Some members of staff genuinely have had some very uncanny experiences.

Speaking on the BBC television series *Battersea Dogs' Home* in the late 1990s, Nightshift Keeper Karen Williams revealed that people had glimpsed strange shadows in Tealby Block, and heard mysterious noises, including footsteps, laughter and the jingling of keys. Karen had never witnessed anything ghostly here herself but another member of staff has.

Just before nine o'clock one Friday night in around 1996, May Whammond was checking the kennels in this block before handing over to the night staff. Tealby is where stray dogs are housed when they first arrive at the home and it contains one hundred and twenty-six kennels arranged on several floors, in four single aisles and one double aisle of kennels per floor. May had already checked the kennels of the first floor and aisles A and B on the second floor and was now just entering the C aisle, which has kennels down both sides. As she walked down between the two rows of kennels she felt the temperature rapidly drop and at about the same time she began to sense something odd about the situation. Normally, whenever somebody walks around the kennels the room echoes to the sound of dogs barking but tonight, she realised, there was absolute silence. Puzzled, she continued walking along the aisle. Nearing the end she happened to glance up at the door – and was startled to see the face of an elderly, grey-haired woman gazing in at her through the door's round window.

'I just stood staring back at it when she smiled at me,' May told me, 'and thinking it was the person that I was working with that night I called out to stop mucking about and that it was

Eland Road, Battersea. (James Clark)

not funny. But the woman's face was still there and still smiling back at me. And the dogs still hadn't barked and the aisle was still cold.'

A sudden fright gripped May and she turned and ran as fast as she could. As she reached the switches she turned out the lights, racing down the stairs in the dark, reasoning that the mysterious woman would not be able to see to follow her. Bursting into the staff area she met the colleague who was on duty with her, together with the two men due to work that night, and she immediately asked if any of them had been 'larking about' upstairs. All replied that they had not. Seeing how obviously distraught May was, the three of them left her to recover in the staff area as they went up to the kennels to search for the intruder. They returned a little later having found nobody and reporting that everything was in order: the temperature was quite normal and the dogs had started barking the moment they opened the door. Perhaps, they gently suggested, May had imagined it, but May is certain she was not mistaken:

> After a while we made a joke of it, but to this day I still believe I did see a woman in the back passage who came to check on the dogs on that night for herself. I now work permanent nights at Battersea and I feel that something is watching me when I do my patrols. I just say out loud, 'It's okay, Mary, just checking the animals and carrying on where you left off.' And I don't get scared like I did on that Friday night.

Another member of staff had an unnerving encounter as she arrived for work early on the morning of 19 October 2005. On this occasion, the setting was nowhere near Tealby Kennels but in a yard that was only acquired by the home relatively recently (within the past fifteen years) and which is used for parking cars and exercising dogs.

Pauline Martignetti is the home's head driver. Her job involves collecting stray dogs and cats from all across London and she has worked here for more than twenty-eight years. She normally travels into work with her husband, another member of staff, but he had to travel to Wales overnight to pick up some dogs to bring back to Battersea and so, unusually, she was on her own as she drove into the yard that morning. She was also a few minutes earlier than usual, and it was around twenty to six in the morning as she passed through the gate.

She left her car briefly to clock in and check the fax machine for the usual messages from police stations that had taken in dogs and cats overnight, then got back into her car, drove up the

yard, parked and let out her own three dogs. Locking the car, she began to walk away and then, for no reason she can identify, she stopped and looked around. In the distance, walking towards her across the yard, was a woman with two small dogs, one on either side of her. There was no doubt whatsoever that the woman was real and physically present, yet there was something not quite right about the scene. The woman had 'a slight Victorian air' about her and it was impossible for Pauline to make out any features of her face or attire as everything about the figure was jet black, like a person seen only in silhouette.

'Who the hell is that?' was Pauline's initial thought, because at that time of the morning the only people that should have been present other than her were the two night men who look after the animals overnight and deal with any public enquiries at the door. This woman should not be there, but Pauline drew some comfort from the fact that the dark figure's two dogs were both clearly secured on leads. Thinking back since that morning, Pauline has racked her brains trying to identify what breed those dogs were but can only conclude they were mongrels. They were just below knee-height with a curly coat, she remembers, 'something like a big Shih-Tzu'.

Pauline had worked at the home for so many years that she was well acquainted with the ghost stories told about the place, and consequently it took just a few seconds of confused thoughts (Who was the woman? What was she doing there? Where was her car?) before it dawned on her that she might be looking at a ghost. Pauline later told me: 'I watched her for several seconds coming towards me then I thought, "Oh, my God, what the hell is that?" My head began to pound as I realised what I was looking at.'

Keen to retreat as quickly as she could, Pauline turned and began to walk away from the apparition. But before she had gone more than ten or fifteen paces, curiosity got the better of her and she turned to see what the woman was doing. The yard was empty.

The entire episode could not have taken much more than ten seconds but Pauline was left quite shaken. Gathering herself as best she could, she hurried to the night staff to ask if anyone

Above: *New Covent Garden Market: an unlikely setting for a ghost. (James Clark)*

Opposite: *Battersea Dogs and Cats Home. (James Clark)*

else was on the premises and only after they confirmed that nobody else was around did she tell them what she had seen. Like Pauline, they were familiar with the stories circulating amongst the staff and so they were less sceptical than might be expected, although they were somewhat surprised it should be Pauline who reported this to them as, despite her many years working at the home, this was the one and only time she has ever made any such claim.

Still feeling nonplussed, Pauline thanked the night staff and walked off to start her day's work. It was not until much later that she remembered that the yard was covered by CCTV cameras. Had they recorded the incident? As soon as she had retrieved the videotape and obtained someone's assistance to help her work the machine, Pauline and four other staff members gathered around the monitor, searching the footage for proof of her strange encounter. They peered eagerly at the screen as Pauline pointed to where the lady should appear. 'Just watch that spot,' she told them. 'Don't take your eyes off that spot.' And just as she said that, all five of them saw an indistinct black shadow pass across the screen, precisely at the point Pauline had indicated. 'I told you, didn't I?' cried Pauline. 'Did I not tell you?'

According to the videotape, Pauline encountered the apparition at five forty-four a.m. but for some reason, getting the tape to that precise point had been extremely tricky and unfortunately this was to be the only time the shadow was seen. Because of the difficulty in finding the right moment, Pauline sought help from someone with expertise in CCTV footage, a friend of hers who works for the transport police. Her friend asked her to bring the tape in and together they spent an entire afternoon searching the footage only for the transport police machine to unexpectedly 'eat' the videotape, the only time this machine has ever malfunctioned in this way. Pauline was able to retrieve the tape and had it repaired by a specialist but since then she has been too nervous to play it, for she has the gnawing suspicion that she is simply not supposed to see the apparition again.

Thinking back now to that October morning, she believes she was granted a rare privilege and wishes she had held her ground to watch the mysterious dark woman for as long as possible:

New Covent Garden Market.
(James Clark)

It wasn't really a frightening experience. She didn't come across as frightening or threatening at all. It was only when I realised what I was looking at that I frightened myself […] I feel it was a great honour for her to show herself to me. My only regret is I turned and walked away. If I could go back I would not move or take my eyes off her.

Fruit and Veg ... and a Ghost

The stalls at New Covent Garden Market might seem an unlikely setting for a ghost, yet that is exactly what a visiting Brighton greengrocer claimed to see here in 1982. That greengrocer was fifty-three-year-old Harold Young. After close of business on the day of his first visit to the fruit and vegetable market, he was startled to see the blood-spattered figure of a man in his sixties or seventies. He was even more shocked when the apparition walked straight through an empty stall and vanished. 'He looked gruesome,' reported Harold, 'he wore a white apron, covered in blood and was carrying a long knife, possibly a meat cleaver. He had sad, sorrowful eyes and stared down at the ground as he walked.'

Harold speculated that the ghost might be that of a murderer or else simply the spirit of an ordinary butcher from long ago. Curiously, despite the blood and knife Harold felt not fear but sympathy towards the figure. His encounter was reported in the *South Western Star* on 7 May 1982. The newspaper sought a comment from the market authority, whose spokesman Ken McKenna was surprised to hear about the sighting, saying: 'We've never heard of ghosts in the market before. It is not the sort of place you would expect to be haunted – it is all concrete and steel here.'

The authority does not seem to have taken the claimed ghostly sighting very seriously, and the story warranted only a brief and dismissive reference in the New Covent Garden Market's newsletter for June/July 1982, which dryly suggested that the knife-wielding figure was: 'Probably just a disgruntled grower come to settle accounts with his trader.'

Chapter Three

PUTNEY

A Putney Poltergeist

For a few weeks in the middle of the twentieth century, the unfortunate occupants of a house in Mexfield Road, East Putney were plagued by poltergeist activity – yet another poltergeist to have targeted Wandsworth Borough!

The house was home to Mr and Mrs Cronin and their three daughters, the twins Joan and Joyce (both twenty-four at the time) and their younger sister June (aged fifteen), and the episode was recorded some years later in a *Wandsworth Borough News* article dated 14 January 1955. Although no precise date was given for these events, the electoral register shows that the Cronins were not living at this address prior to the Second World War but had moved in by 1945; as the 1955 article makes no reference to the events taking place during the war, it would seem that this poltergeist probably showed up sometime between 1945 and the early 1950s.

The poltergeist first made its presence known in the back bedroom where one of the twins, Joan, was woken one night by noises coming from her bed. As she lay listening to the eerie scratches and bangs, she grew increasingly frightened until at last she cried out for her father. When Mr Cronin rushed in to find out what was wrong, Joan persuaded him to knock on the wall to see what happened. Naturally sceptical when it came to the supernatural, Mr Cronin knocked four times and was startled to receive four knocks in reply.

Joan continued to sleep in the bedroom for another few nights but as the mysterious noises became louder and more insistent she moved into the kitchen, hoping to find some peace there. She was to be disappointed, for the sounds simply followed her into that room. Unsure what to do, Mr Cronin tried involving the police but they were convinced he was imagining things and offered no help. To make matters worse, it seemed as if the poltergeist was growing in strength: the noises now came during the day as well as at night and some strange energy had started to move objects around.

Small items including hairpins and eggcups were thrown from the dresser, and a Christmas card that had been left on that dresser was found on the floor, screwed up into a ball. Items left in one location would vanish and reappear somewhere else and it was even claimed that the

Mexfield Road, East Putney. (James Clark)

dining table rose into the air. On one particularly bizarre occasion, an orange was discovered inside the teapot. 'Once I was powdering my face,' said Joan, 'and a box of chocolates lay on the dressing-table. Suddenly I found a chocolate in the powder-box. Every time I woke up there was a book lying in the bed.' Joan also claimed that 'you could sense there was a coldness in the room' whenever the poltergeist was present.

The poltergeist's antics became so disruptive that Joan's twin sister Joyce suffered a nervous breakdown and had to be admitted to hospital. Their younger sister, the teenage June, was also victimised. She complained of something invisible touching her and said that some force would pull down the wires of the bedspring as she lay in bed at night, and lift her blanket into the air. The strange happenings affected June badly and she became so pale and thin that her appearance shocked her schoolteacher when he called at her home one day to deliver some photographs.

Mr J.A. Gilbrook knew June well because she was in his class at Southfields Secondary School, and he was prepared to believe her extraordinary story. 'She was the last girl I would suspect of imagining things,' he commented, 'for she had her feet firmly planted on the ground. The subject of ghosts came up in class before the poltergeist arrived on the scene, and she had firmly stated that she did not believe in them.'

Gilbrook was a committed Christian. He was a former missionary and a lay reader of the Church of England, and his natural reaction was to arrange for an exorcism to be performed. He assisted in this himself, together with the Reverend R. Fletcher Tink, American minister of the Church of the Nazarene in Battersea, and the Reverend J. Crouch, minister of the Church of the Nazarene in West Norwood, who had prior experience with such matters. One by one, each of the three men said a prayer of exorcism and commanded the poltergeist to depart in the name of Jesus Christ.

Right: *St Mary the Virgin church, Putney. (James Clark)*

Below: *Putney Bridge spanning the River Thames: Fulham is to the left, Putney to the right. (James Clark)*

The exorcism apparently worked for, according to Mr Gilbrook: 'From that day to this the family has never had any further trouble with the poltergeist.'

The Church that Giants Built

The site of St Mary the Virgin church at the southern end of Putney Bridge has been used for Christian worship since at least the thirteenth century. Excavations have shown that a building may have existed here even earlier, in the eleventh or twelfth centuries, but nobody is certain precisely when the first church was established, nor who built it. One odd story, however, purports to tell us not only who built the church, but also the origin of the names Putney and Fulham.

Apparently, St Mary the Virgin was built at the same time as All Saints church in Fulham (which stands at the opposite end of the bridge), and the builders were a pair of sisters. The sisters possessed only one hammer between them, and this would be flung across the river in response to a pre-arranged cry:

> ...those on the Surrey side made use of the word, put it nigh! Those on the opposite shore, heave it full home! whence the churches, and from them the villages, were called Putnigh and Fullhome, since corrupted to Putney and Fulham.

This charming legend appears in Francis Grose's *Provincial Glossary* of 1787 and is, according to Jennifer Westwood in her *Albion: A Guide to Legendary Britain*, 'a cheerful variation of one commonly told of giants'. Because of this, Westwood speculates that the sisters who supposedly built these churches were themselves giantesses. For those who find this legendary explanation too much to accept, John Field, in his *Place Names of Greater London* suggests the following alternative derivations for the towns' names, both of which come from Old English (the language spoken and written by Anglo-Saxons):

Fulham: 'Fulla's riverside pasture'

Putney: 'Putta's quay or landing place'

St Mary the Virgin church can claim not only a legend about giantesses but also a ghost story. The apparition is said to be of a mysterious crouching figure that haunts the churchyard. In another version of this tale, the crouching figure is briefly seen on Putney Bridge, close to the church, but when the witness looks back the bridge is deserted.

The White Lady of Ranelagh

The story of the White Lady of Ranelagh begins with a murder. As a lady and her lover kept tryst one night in the grounds of Old Ranelagh, a jealous rival for the lady's affections stabbed the lover in the back, killing him. Since that fateful night, whenever the moon is full the killer's restless spirit gallops his ghostly horse away south and out onto the Lower Richmond Road in Putney, to be followed a short while later by the spectre of a lady in white. She walks slowly and sadly, weeping and calling out the name of her murdered lover: 'Paul, Paul!'

Lower Richmond Road, Putney. (James Clark)

Barn Elms Playing Fields. (James Clark)

The grounds of Old Ranelagh lay on the south side of the Thames close to the extreme north-western border of Wandsworth Borough, on land that once belonged to a large manor house called Barn Elms. (Traces of that name can be seen on maps today, for example in 'Barn Elms Playing Fields' and 'Barn Elms School Sports Centre'.) In 1884, the Ranelagh Club moved into the premises after their lease of Ranelagh House in Fulham expired, and the venue became well known for polo matches. In 1939, the army took over the house, ruining the interior in the process, and the building later stood empty until eventually being demolished after fire gutted it in 1954.

It may be that the story of the White Lady stems from a true episode of 1668 recounted by Samuel Pepys in his famous diary. George Villiers, the second Duke of Buckingham and a man notorious for his intrigues and immorality, was having an affair with the Countess of Shrewsbury, Anna Maria. The Countess's wronged husband – Francis Talbot, the eleventh Earl of Shrewsbury – ill-advisedly challenged Buckingham to a duel, in the course of which he was badly injured. He died shortly afterwards. In his entry for 17 January 1668, Pepys records hearing of: '… the Duel yesterday between the Duke of Buckingham, Holmes, and one Jenkins, on one side, and my Lord of Shrewsbury, Sir Jo. Talbot, and one Bernard Howard, on the other side: and all about my Lady Shrewsbury, who is a whore, and is at this time, and hath for a great while been, a whore to the Duke of Buckingham; and so her husband challenged him, and they met yesterday in a close near Barne-Elmes, and there fought: and my Lord Shrewsbury is run through the body, from the right breast through the shoulder: and Sir Jo. Talbot all along up one of his armes; and Jenkins killed upon the place, and the rest all, in a little measure, wounded.'

The Countess is supposed to have attended the duel herself, disguised as a page boy looking after Buckingham's horse, and she may very well be the historical figure who later became the phantom 'White Lady' of legend, the original events having become distorted. But before dismissing the ghost story as nothing but local folklore, it should be noted that at least one person has claimed first-hand experience of this haunting.

In a letter to the *Wandsworth Borough News* published on 7 January 1955, John Sluter told how as a boy he and four friends once talked themselves into looking for the phantom lady and horseman. Climbing through a gap in the fence behind Putney Hospital, they broke into the polo grounds and made their way to the drive. There, they found a large tree to hide behind and waited. They had deliberately chosen a night with a full moon but the heavy shadows cast by the trees around them cloaked their hiding place in darkness.

Faraway, the clock at Putney Bridge tolled the first hour past midnight, and still the boys continued their vigil. Each of them was scared, cold and tired and if truth were told would rather be at home in bed, but none wanted to admit as much in front of the others and so all four remained silently waiting…

> Then suddenly from the bottom of the drive came a sound, a furious rushing, a pounding of hooves, and through the gates and into the road swept a horseman … but the horse and the man were invisible and, worst of all, the gates stayed locked and closed.

This was too much for the four young ghost-hunters. Terrified, they fled, racing back down the drive, through the gap in the fence and homeward to the comfort of their beds, leaving the mystery of the White Lady of Ranelagh behind them for more foolhardy souls to investigate.

Putney's Haunted Heath

The wild expanse of Putney Heath and Wimbledon Common was once a very dangerous place for travellers. What is now Putney Heath Lane used to be known as 'Cutthroat Lane' (see, for example, the 1874 Ordnance Survey map) and it was a brave, or foolish, person who journeyed alone across the heath itself, haunted as it was by highwaymen and their pedestrian equivalents, the footpads. The ghost of one of these highwaymen is said to haunt the Heath still.

At the end of the eighteenth century, the old Portsmouth Road running through here was a major coaching route carrying travellers between London and Portsmouth. The journey was an uncomfortable one as the cramped coaches rattled and bounced their way along the rough, pitted lanes, and conditions were made worse by the constant fear of attack. In particular, the

The derelict Putney Hospital. (James Clark)

lonely stretch of the route crossing Putney Heath was a favourite hunting ground of one of the most notorious of all highwaymen: Jerry Abershaw.

Born in Kingston in 1773, by the age of seventeen Abershaw was already the leader of his own gang of highway robbers. It was always likely he would fulfil his mother's prophecy that he would die with his boots on. Despite his relative youth, though, Abershaw bore little resemblance to the dashing highwaymen of romantic legend. He and his later companion Dick Ferguson were once described by a Hounslow innkeeper as 'terrible, cursing and swearing, and thrusting the muzzles of their pistols into people's mouths' and according to the *Newgate Calendar* Abershaw was 'one of the most fierce, depraved, and infamous of the human race.'

From 1790, there was a noticeable increase in the number of local highway robberies, and this has been attributed to Abershaw's arrival on the scene. His infamy spread rapidly. A popular saying of the period compared Abershaw to the then-Prime Minister, saying that 'Abershaw takes their purses with pistols – Pitt with Parliament'.

The journey between London and Portsmouth was a long one of more than seventy miles (113 kilometres) and coaches would make several stops at inns along the route, to change horses and to allow travellers to refresh themselves and perhaps rest overnight. Such stops were necessary but they also added to the danger of the journey because some of the more cunning highwaymen might well be lurking within, observing who entered and assessing the wealth of potential prey. The Green Man public house on Putney Heath, for example, was frequented by highwaymen and footpads, and today a sign depicting a highwayman hangs above the nearby roundabout at Tibbet's Corner (see 'The Highwayman Who Never Existed', page 55).

Abershaw himself, however, operated out of an inn named the Baldfaced Stag. This inn, which no longer exists, stood on the old Portsmouth Road in Putney Vale, at the junction of modern day Roehampton Vale and Stag Lane.

The entrance to 'Cutthroat Lane' today. (James Clark)

Putney Heath: once the hunting ground of Jerry Abershaw. (James Clark)

The Green Man, Putney Heath. (James Clark)

Abershaw evaded capture for five long years but in 1795 two Bow Street Runners, David Price and Bernard Turner, received information that he was at the Three Brewers public house in Southwark and went to arrest him. As they approached, recorded the *Newgate Calendar*, Abershaw 'placed himself at the entrance to the parlour with a loaded pistol in each hand, vowing the instant death of any one who should attempt to take him.' In the ensuing battle Price was shot and killed but Abershaw was captured and on 30 July 1795 the villain was at last brought to trial at the Croydon assizes where he was found guilty of murder. The *Newgate Calendar* recorded his reaction to this sentence in lurid detail:

> When the judge appeared in the black cap [...] Avershaw [sic], with the most unbridled insolence and bravado, clapped his hat upon his head, and pulled up his breeches with a vulgar swagger; and during the whole of the ceremony, which deeply affected all present except the senseless object himself, he stared full in the face of the judge with a malicious sneer and affected contempt, and continued this conduct till he was taken, bound hand and foot, from the dock, venting curses and insults on the judge and jury for having consigned him to 'murder'.

His execution was carried out on Kennington Common on 3 August 1795 and took place, said the *Newgate Calendar*, 'in the presence of an immense multitude of spectators, among whom he recognised many acquaintances and confederates, to whom he bowed, nodded, and laughed with the most unfeeling indifference. He had a flower in his mouth, and his waistcoat and shirt were unbuttoned, leaving his bosom open in the true style of vulgar gaiety; and, talking to the mob, and venting curses on the officers, he died, as he had lived, a ruffian and a brute!' In one

The Baldfaced Stag inn stood at the junction of Roehampton Vale and Stag Lane. (James Clark)

final act of defiance, Abershaw reportedly kicked off his boots during his execution to disprove his mother's prophecy.

After his corpse was cut down, it was taken to Wimbledon Common to be gibbeted. Gibbeting involved publicly displaying the bodies of executed criminals by hanging them in chains or in a cage. The bodies were often coated in pitch so that they would be preserved longer, prolonging the impact of this powerful visual warning to others not to follow the criminal's path. Abershaw's gibbet was constructed especially to overlook the area he had terrorised for half a decade.

Huge numbers of people flocked to see the gruesome spectacle. Johnny Townsend (another Bow Street Runner and the organiser of Abershaw's execution) estimated that as many as 100,000 people visited the site, which gives some idea of the notoriety Abershaw had achieved. On the first night, Townsend was forced to keep watch with ten men following rumours of a plot to steal the corpse. That attempt was never made, but ghouls did later help themselves to various 'souvenirs', the *Newgate Calendar* recording how they 'procured from his decaying and piece-meal carcass the bones of his fingers and toes to convert into stoppers for their tobacco-pipes.'

In his 1834 book *Jacob Faithful*, local writer Captain Frederick Marryat described an encounter with this gibbet. The eponymous Jacob had become lost on Wimbledon Common during a snowstorm and as the clouds rolled away to reveal a clear, star-filled sky:

> The first object which caught my eye was a post within two yards of us. I looked at it, followed it up with my eyes, and, to my horror, beheld a body suspended and swinging in chains over our heads ... As soon as I recovered from the shock which the first view occasioned, I pointed it out to Tom, who had not yet moved. He looked up, started back, and fell over the dog

— jumped up again, and burst out into as loud a laugh as his frozen jaws would permit. 'It's old Jerry Abershaw,' said he, 'I know him well, and now I know where we are.' This was the case; Abershaw had, about three years before, been hung in chains on Wimbledon Common; and the unearthly sound we had heard was the creaking of the rusty iron as the body was swung to-and-fro by the gale.

The site of the gibbet is still known as Jerry's Hill and is located on Wimbledon Common a short distance to the northeast of Putney Vale Cemetery. A nearby pond is also named after him: Jerry's Pond (shown on some maps as the Curling pond).

The gibbet and its grisly burden have long since vanished, but legend has it that Jerry Abershaw's ghost still roams across Putney Heath and Wimbledon Common. According to Peter Underwood in his *Haunted London*, the spectral highwayman is supposed to gallop his steed here at night, while an article in the *Wandsworth Borough News* of 23 December 1976 states that on dark and windy nights a figure resembling Abershaw can sometimes be seen on foot here and that his phantom steed stands nearby, pawing the ground and whimpering as it awaits the return of its master. This second version of the story bears a strong similarity to a ghost story that is told about an old house called Colebrook Lodge that once stood near here. (See 'The Spectral Horse of Colebrook Lodge', page 58.) Abershaw's ghost even receives a brief mention in George Borrow's 1851 novel, *Lavengro*:

> Did not Mr Petulengro mention one Jemmy Abershaw? Yes. Did he not tell me that the life and adventures of Jemmy Abershaw would bring in much money to the writer? Yes, but I knew nothing of that worthy. I heard, it is true, from Mr Petulengro, that when alive he committed robberies on the hill, on the side of which Mr Petulengro had pitched his tents, and that his ghost still haunted the hill at midnight; but those were scant materials out of which to write the man's life.

Jerry Abershaw also features as a character in a fictional tale of the supernatural written by T.G. Jackson. Called 'The Red House', this was published in 1919 as part of a collection entitled *Six Ghost Stories*. (A fuller account of Jerry Abershaw's life and exploits is given in Clive Whichelow's booklet *Local Highwaymen*.)

For ghost-hunters not content with a mere highwayman, there is also a story that the headless spectre of King Charles I gallops past Putney Heath along the old Portsmouth Road. Would-be witnesses are advised to wrap up warmly though, as this apparition is supposed to appear at midnight on 30 January, the anniversary of his beheading.

The Highwayman Who Never Existed

Looming menacingly above the roundabout at Tibbet's Corner is the silhouetted figure of a highwayman leaning forward with pistol drawn. This striking image has helped to continue the popular myth that Tibbet's Corner takes its name from a highwayman who used to operate around here. Although this area really was once infested by highwaymen, explaining the image's design, this is not where the name comes from. The true story is that a building at the entrance to the Wimbledon Park estate of Earl Spencer (lord of the manor during the nineteenth century) was occupied by a Mrs Thibet; her son became one of the estate gamekeepers, the family name became anglicised to Tibbet and people came to know the area as 'Tibbet's Corner'.

Another oft-repeated claim is that Tibbet's Corner was once a site of execution. It is likely that this belief stems from the similarity in sound between 'Tibbet' and 'gibbet', gibbeting being the practice of hanging the corpse of an executed criminal in chains or in a cage to serve as a warning to others. A *Wandsworth Borough News* article of 15 January 1937, for example, informed readers that: 'The name, 'Tibbet's Corner', where seven roads converge at the top of West Hill, is considered to be a corruption of "Gibbet Corner".'

As has been stated, this is not where the name really comes from, but perhaps there is some truth in the idea that criminals have been punished around here in the past. In the stables of Colebrook Lodge on West Hill were once kept some rusty chains and manacles, which according to tradition were relics of summary judgement. Unfortunately, they were lost when that old building was demolished. (See 'The Spectral Horse of Colebrook Lodge', page 58, for another ghost story from this area.)

The two beliefs described above are often combined in the myth that Tibbet's Corner roundabout stands on the site where Tibbet – the highwayman who never existed – was publicly hanged.

At the end of the twentieth century, Tibbet's Corner was momentarily caught up in the space-age mystery of UFOs, according to a report in *UFO Roundup* of 13 July 1997. A little after noon on Saturday 5 July 1997, Alex Maddern and his wife glanced out of the kitchen window of their fourth-floor apartment near Tibbet's Corner and spotted a 'very strange object moving across the sky.' The 'metallic disk' was 'clam-shaped' with a highly reflective surface like polished aluminium, and remained in sight for approximately half a minute as it travelled across the bright, cloudless sky in the direction of Kingston. Was this merely the misidentification of a plane, or something stranger?

Above: *Looking south towards Tibbet's Corner roundabout. (James Clark)*

Right: *The image of a highwayman hangs above Tibbet's Corner roundabout. (James Clark)*

Opposite: *Portsmouth Road, Putney Heath. (James Clark)*

The road name is a reminder of the grand house that once stood here. (James Clark)

The Spectral Horse of Colebrook Lodge

Immediately to the northeast of Tibbet's Corner is a triangle of land bounded by Tibbet's Ride/ Putney Hill, Putney Heath Lane and West Hill. Within this triangle once stood a grand old house known as Colebrook Lodge. According to legend, Oliver Cromwell lived at Colebrook Lodge for a time during the English Civil Wars, while he was using Putney Church as his 'headquarters' (presumably during the Putney Debates of 1647). This seems unlikely to be true, however, not least because Colebrook Lodge did not exist then. The turmoil of the English Civil Wars lasted from 1642 until 1651 but it was not until the late 1780s that Sir William Fordyce had a large house built here and named it Colebrook Lodge. It was an impressive building and the 'Local Enq. File' at Wandsworth Local History Service contains an 1834 description of the house that gives a clear impression of what it was like by the first half of the nineteenth century:

> PUTNEY-HEATH. – To be LET, in a perfect state of repair and fit for the immediate reception of a family of distinction, Colebrook Lodge; containing entrance hall, breakfast, dining, and gentleman's rooms, library and billiard rooms, with a spacious and elegant drawing room commanding extensive views, 12 bed rooms, 3 water closets, and offices of all descriptions; stabling for 6 horses with coachman's rooms over, 2 coach-houses, and other out-buildings; also a productive kitchen garden, flower garden, and 3 paddocks of excellent grass land, altogether 15 acres, with additional land if required.

The estate was probably split up around the 1880s as large houses were being built in this area, and by May 1935 Colebrook Lodge was empty and awaiting demolition. It was eventually pulled down to make way for the flats of Colebrook Close.

Although the old house no longer exists it leaves behind a romantic ghost story, of a spectral horse that supposedly haunted the stables. The story is that a highwayman once left his horse tethered here, intending to come back for it later, but shortly afterwards was captured and later executed by hanging at 'Gibbett Corner'. (See 'The Highwayman Who Never Existed, page 55, for the true story behind 'Gibbett Corner'.) His loyal steed waits forever for the return of its long-dead master, pawing at the ground and whinnying as it listens out for the footsteps that will never come.

Chapter Four

TOOTING

Thomas Hardy: The Return of the Novelist?

On the wall of No. 172 Trinity Road in Tooting hangs a blue plaque stating that this building was once home to the great poet and novelist Thomas Hardy (1840–1928), author of such classics as *Far From the Madding Crowd* and *The Return of the Native*. Something not mentioned on the plaque is that Hardy may still reside here, at least in spirit.

In a newspaper article about homes with interesting histories (*The Express*, 2 October 1999), Felicity Hope – then a resident here – revealed how a young lady from one of the building's lower flats was startled by what she believed was Hardy's ghost: '[One] of the girls who lived downstairs was convinced she had seen his ghost. She got hysterical one night, when she thought he'd walked through her kitchen.'

When Thomas Hardy and his wife Emma moved here in 1878 the house had a different name and number, being known as No. 1 Arundel Terrace. The couple lived here until 1881. During his Tooting years Hardy wrote *The Trumpet Major* and *A Laodicean*, and his connection with the area is recalled in the title of his beautiful and haunting poem, *Beyond the Last Lamp (Near Tooting Common)*. Their stay here was not a happy one though, as this was a period of serious illness for Hardy and the couple eventually left London for a healthier life away from the metropolis.

Today, the house has been split into three flats over four floors. The top flat consists of the upper two floors, the middle flat the first floor, and the third flat is technically the basement flat although it is actually at ground level at the rear of the property.

In 2003, I got in touch with the occupiers of these flats and one of them, Craig Marcham, confirmed that he was aware of the story about Hardy's ghost. As he recalled, he probably heard it originally from Felicity Hope who was still living in another of the flats when he and his girlfriend moved in in 2001. The ghostly encounter took place in the kitchen of either the first floor or ground floor flats, and Craig believes it most likely to have been on the first floor. He described how an extension at the rear of the property provides an extra room for each of these flats, and commented:

Left: *Thomas Hardy's old house in Tooting. (James Clark)*

Below: *Plaque on the wall of 172 Trinity Road, Tooting. (James Clark)*

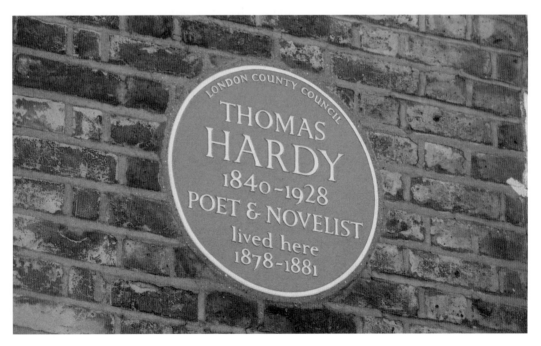

This extension was only built in the 1970s or '80s and I doubt therefore that Hardy would choose to haunt a room that wasn't even built when he lived in the house. In [the ground floor flat] this modern extension is the kitchen whereas in the first floor flat the modern extension is a bathroom and the kitchen therefore is part of the original Victorian house. On that basis I think it more likely that Felicity was referring to the kitchen in the first floor flat.

Although he has never seen any sign of a ghost himself, Craig did mention two slightly odd incidents that occurred since he moved in:

A painting hung on the living room wall fell down in the middle of the night once and about a month later three glass shelves which were supporting four large glass jars and about six glasses fell down in the kitchen. Unremarkable in itself but strangely both events occurred at roughly the same time in the night (between two and two-thirty) and on both occasions nothing actually smashed.

He is 'slightly sceptical' when it comes to ghosts however, and so is disinclined to view these events as anything more than coincidence. Indeed, if it had not been for the reported ghost sighting he would have given no further thought to the matter at all.

Bearing in mind Hardy's unhappy time in this house, it is maybe difficult to understand why his ghost would have returned. On the other hand, as the following extract from a conversation with William Archer (*Pall Mall Magazine*, April 1901) suggests, he might not have been totally averse to the idea:

(Hardy): I am most anxious to believe in what, roughly speaking, we may call the supernatural – but I find no evidence for it! People accuse me of scepticism, materialism, and so forth; but, if the accusation is just at all, it is quite against my will. For instance, I seriously assure you that I would give ten years of my life – well, perhaps that offer is rather beyond my means – but when I was a younger man, I would cheerfully have given ten years of my life to see a ghost – an authentic, indubitable spectre.

Given such sentiments perhaps he would rather have enjoyed the prospect of revisiting his old home in spectral form!

The Phantom Smacker of Marius Road

During the 1950s, a young lad was the unwilling victim of a ghostly bully. Whenever he passed a particular cupboard in the hallway at his home in Marius Road, 'Peter' (pseudonym) felt something smack him around the legs. Occasionally, the same thing happened while Peter was in his room, which was located opposite the same cupboard. The smacking was bad enough as it was, but to make matters worse the culprit was invisible!

The unseen assailant began its persecution when Peter was about four years old and continued for around six years. Unsurprisingly nobody would ever believe the boy's fantastic tale. As Peter's son-in-law 'Michael' (pseudonym) told me: 'Everyone thought he was mad but he swears that it was definitely a smack.'

Marius Road, Tooting. (James Clark)

'It Was Like a Horror Movie...'

In November 1988, Jan Love moved into a four-bedroom council flat in Haddenham Court in Tooting's Hazelhurst Road. Almost as soon as she arrived, the single mother of four sensed there was something not quite right about her new home.

For the first few days, Jan was troubled by nothing more than 'bad feelings' but then one night she awoke in terror to find herself pinned to the bed. Sitting astride her chest and pressing down with its hands was the apparition of a woman whose long black hair flew wildly about her head as if blown by some unfelt gale. 'It was like a horror movie,' Jan later told the *Wandsworth Borough News* (17 August 1990).

This type of experience, often known as the 'Old Hag', is more common than might be thought and has been linked to a condition known as sleep paralysis. However, other events reported around the same time cast doubt on such a psychological explanation. It was claimed, for example, that bolts for hanging pot plants became detached by themselves, that light bulbs exploded and that on one occasion, Jan was redecorating the bathroom when some strange force grabbed the paint remover right out of her hands.

Particularly badly affected was Jan's youngest daughter, four-year-old Amy, who often woke screaming that a man was beating her. Events took an even more sinister turn one day when a door suddenly came away from the wardrobe. It crashed down onto the bed and would have landed on Amy had it not been for the quick reactions of a family friend who snatched the little girl to safety.

One evening, Jan's twenty-five-year-old sister Carmen and a friend came to visit. As they sat chatting, there was a knock at the door and when Jan went to answer it the stereo suddenly switched on, all by itself. 'Something is wrong with the house,' Carmen said later. 'I would not live there.'

In around March of 1990, Jan started to suffer health problems. Her hair began to fall out and a visit to the hospital revealed that her liver showed signs of excessive alcohol consumption. This baffled Jan as she did not drink, but it seemed to be connected with a neighbour's theory about the ghost's identity. When she heard Jan's description of the black-haired apparition, this neighbour suggested it was the spirit of a reclusive alcoholic named Isabel Weldon. According to the neighbour, an elderly couple had previously occupied the flat and had employed Isabel

Haddenham Court, Tooting.
(James Clark)

as a live-in housekeeper. After the couple died, Isabel had continued to live there with her pet spaniel, until one night she died in her sleep. Her body, and the near-starving spaniel, had remained undiscovered in the flat for five days.

Jan consulted a psychic, who agreed that the flat was haunted and claimed to sense the spirit of a lonely old woman who had not been ready to die and who was searching for her lost son. The entity, she said, was frightened but not evil. It would, however, continue to 'feed' off Jan and her family unless they made it quite clear that the flat belonged to them now and that Isabel was no longer welcome.

Understandably, Jan asked to be moved to a different council flat and in August 1990 was informed that her application had been successful. But she was less than pleased to learn that the flat the council now proposed to give her was on an estate she considered unsuitable for raising a family. Balancing her options, she decided to stay where she was and take her chances with the ghost instead.

The Tunnel, the Ghost and the 'Resurrection Men'

St Nicholas' church in Church Lane is a tall, elegant building in the Gothic style that stands a little way back from the main road and can sometimes be overlooked amidst the hustle and bustle of modern-day Tooting. Built in the nineteenth century and consecrated by the Bishop of Winchester in February 1833, the present church is not the first to stand here. The grounds have been a site of worship for at least the last thousand years: there was a Saxon building here in the eleventh century and there are records of a Christian community existing as far back as the seventh century.

A Secret Tunnel

There is also a legend of a secret tunnel leading from the old Saxon church (which stood behind where the present church now stands) and running underground to a building in a nearby field. This small building may have been home to a colony of Brethren of the Holy Cross. 'Here, then,' wrote Walford in his *Greater London: A Narrative of its History, its People, and its Places* (1884), 'on the ground now in great measure covered by dwellings abutting on the road which is known as the Vant Road, stood, in what must have been the seclusion and quiet of perfect country, the moated monastery of which no known trace now remains.'

It is possible that the moat was used as a sort of fishpond but its primary purpose was protection, safeguarding the brethren against the robbers 'who infested the lonely country lanes and roads around London', according to W.E. Morden in *The History of Tooting-Graveney*, Surrey (1897). This ever-present danger also supplies a rationale for the supposed tunnel; it may have been constructed as a means of passing between the monastery and church without being observed.

The possible existence of a tunnel here was recorded by Mr James Barringer, a local baker and notary, in the *Parish Magazine* of 1884. Barringer believed that the subterranean passage had once led from the old church 'to a monastery in the meadow behind the School.' In April 2005 the Reverend Christopher J. Davis told me that the school in question may have been a small village school that stood in Church Lane, just over the road from the church itself and, if so, the supposed tunnel need only have been around 100 yards (ninety-one metres) long.

The origin of the tunnel story is not definitely known but one suggestion is that it is no more than a romantic legend born when the Bateman tomb was raised and an old drain was discovered running under the road. During the time of the Reverend Derek Keppel (1914–1938), that section of the churchyard was thoroughly searched for evidence of the tunnel but none was found. More recently however, according to information passed to me by the Reverend Davis, Eric Hersee reported observing the so-called 'tunnel' or 'drain' when foundations were laid for the Day Centre for the elderly (erected in 1980) that stands next to the churchyard today.

The old Saxon church was demolished in 1834. The rubble was used to fill in the medieval moat that lay along the north side of Church Lane and it is just possible that fragments of that ancient church still exist beneath the road's surface.

Seeking Lost Treasure

In the late 1920s, an elderly gentleman had a particularly vivid dream. In it, he saw a group of monks hastily hiding their valuables in the hidden tunnel, before sealing the opening and departing in haste. This gentleman was quite sure that lifting a particular large gravestone behind St Nicholas' church would reveal secret steps leading down to the subterranean passageway.

Accompanied by a columnist for the *Tooting Gazette*, who wrote under the name 'The Sphinx', he entered the churchyard late one night and together the two men made their way to the gravestone, which lay embedded flat in the ground. But the pair had come poorly equipped for their task and wasted so much time trying to lift the stone without proper tools that their supply of matches ran out, leaving them quite literally in the dark.

As they stood in the oppressive blackness among the graves, the night silent save for the dry rustling of leaves, the reality of their surroundings slowly began to creep up on them. Suddenly, they both distinctly heard a 'quiet chuckle' from somewhere nearby. The Sphinx's nerve broke and he raced away, abandoning his companion. It was only after he left the churchyard and caught sight of a courting couple that he realised from where the laughter had actually come!

'The Ghost of Tooting Churchyard'

In another *Tooting Gazette* article (26 May 1928), The Sphinx told how several people had recently asked him if he knew about 'the ghost of Tooting Churchyard': 'The ghost, so they told me, sits on the top of a grave overrun with weeds and neglected, at the head of which is

Right: *St Nicholas' church, Tooting. (James Clark)*

Below: *Church Lane, Tooting. (James Clark)*

*St Nicholas' churchyard, Tooting.
(James Clark)*

a tombstone. On the stone is inscribed the well-known words, "Gone but not forgotten: never shall thy memory fade!"'

Light-heartedly, he suggested that the ghost might be that of a Mrs Thumber who lived in Tooting in around 1830. Mrs Thumber, whom he rather unkindly described as 'a busybody with nothing else to do but to go into people's houses and learn all about their business' had attended church regularly and taken great pleasure in walking around the neat little churchyard, with its well-maintained graves.

Sadly, by 1928, the churchyard was no longer the pretty place it had once been. Graves had fallen into disrepair, areas were waterlogged, and the rector had decreed that there was no room for further burials. Maybe, opined The Sphinx, it was the decay of a place she had once loved that so troubled Mrs Thumber's restless spirit.

The 'Resurrection Men'

On a darker note, perhaps the story of a ghost in the churchyard is somehow connected with the 'resurrection men' – or body-snatchers – who once operated here. This is why there used to be a sentry box in the churchyard, from which a guard could keep vigil over the newly-dug graves.

Dissecting human bodies to understand how they work is an important part of medical training but prior to the 1832 Anatomy Act the only corpses the medical profession could legally procure were those of hanged murderers, which averaged only 20 to 30 per year. Nobody in that age would voluntarily leave their body to science, because of the widespread belief that being buried incomplete would cost you your place in Heaven, and so the medical profession's demand for the resurrectionists' services was great.

In an article originally written in 1884 and published in the *Tooting Gazette* on 16 May 1931, one local resident recalled how, some years before the old Saxon church was demolished, body-snatchers would often come in the night to 'unearth the grave of a recently buried corpse and take the body away as they found a ready sale for it at a doctor's in London for dissecting purposes.'

The same author remembered how the body of one young girl, whose parents he knew well, had been carried away in the night and how her discarded blue coffin had remained in the belfry for many years until the old church was finally pulled down.

Chapter Five

WANDSWORTH

Spooks at the Royal Victoria Patriotic Building

The Royal Victoria Patriotic Building has known both types of spook, the government variety as well as the ghostly sort. Looming above Fitzhugh Grove, just off Trinity Road and on the edge of Wandsworth Common, this imposing neo-Gothic masterpiece looks so dramatic that some have cheekily called it 'Dracula's Castle', but the flippant reference hardly seems necessary: this building already has plenty of strange stories to tell.

A Home for Orphan Girls

Its original name was the Royal Victoria Patriotic Asylum, a title that has fooled many into believing this was once an institution for the mentally ill. In fact, the money for this building came from the Patriotic Fund set up in 1854 for the relief of dependants of servicemen killed during the Crimean War. The asylum's declared purpose was the 'education and training of three hundred orphan daughters of soldiers, seamen and marines who perished in the Russian War, and for those who hereafter may require like succour'. Land was purchased from Earl Spencer and on 11 July 1857, Queen Victoria herself laid the foundation stone. The following year saw the completion of the initial phase of building and the first inmates were received on 1 July 1859. There were one hundred and fifty to begin with, and that number eventually doubled.

Life for the young orphan girls was tough. Their heads were shaved to prevent lice and each morning they were hosed down with cold water in one of the courtyards. Warming up afterwards must have been difficult in winter because the girls' dormitories were unheated. The orphans' duties included pumping water by hand from an underground supply up to the water tanks in the towers, as well as doing all the laundry, cleaning and cooking, and discipline was harsh. It is this last aspect of the orphans' lives that underlies the best-known ghost story from this building, but that story will be covered later.

The Royal Victoria Patriotic Building. (James Clark)

A First World War hospital

In 1914, at the outbreak of what would become known as the First World War, while the girls were away on holiday, the building's function suddenly changed. Prior to the war, plans had been drawn up for the creation of four Territorial Force General Hospitals in London, and so when the fighting began the Royal Victoria Patriotic Asylum became the South Western General Hospital. A temporary railway station was constructed in front of the building so that trains could bring in wounded soldiers, and as the war dragged on and casualties mounted huts were erected around the main building to provide additional capacity. At its height, the hospital was treating 1,800 patients.

After the war, the orphan school moved back into the asylum and it remained there until world events intervened once again. Following the Munich Crisis of 1938, with imminent war against the Nazis darkening the future, the school was evacuated to Wales. It would never return to Wandsworth, moving instead to premises in Hertfordshire where it eventually closed in 1972.

The Second World War: Secrets and Spies

In September 1939, Hitler's troops invaded Poland, Britain declared war on Germany and a fascinating but secretive chapter in this building's history was about to begin. For several years previously, vast numbers of German refugees had been arriving in Britain and as the German Blitzkrieg now began to roll across Europe, more refugees started to pour in from the Continent. With all these new arrivals, the country had to be on the alert for enemy spies. Under the Aliens Order, most foreign nationals from enemy countries were interned while those from other countries had to be cleared by the authorities. To begin with though, this vetting procedure was far from perfect, performed under improvised conditions and often consisting of little more than an examining officer (known as a 'B.24') looking through a list of names. A better system was drastically needed.

The decision was taken to set up a central screening establishment so that all arrivals would be processed under one roof. So, in January 1941 the Internment Camps Division of the Home Office took over the premises of what was by now known as the Royal Victoria Patriotic School. Under a directive from Section D4 of MI5, all incoming travellers from Allied and friendly countries (with very few exceptions, such as high-ranking Allied officers, or those with valid diplomatic papers) would from now on be sent here for questioning. (Female refugees were housed separately but nearby, in a building in Nightingale Lane.)

Technically, this new centre was under Home Office control, but in practice it was run by the espionage section of MI5 (subsection B.1.D.). As well as trying to intercept enemy spies before they could send intelligence back to the Germans, staff were on the lookout for potential recruits for Britain's own covert organisations and to this end the MI5 officers stationed here were joined by officers from SIS (Secret Intelligence Service, aka MI6) and SOE (Special Operations Executive).

The School opened for its new role on 10 January 1941 and processed 155 foreign nationals in its first month. This figure rose quickly and sharply, to an average of 700 per month. April 1941 saw the arrival of Lt-Col. Oreste Pinto as Head of Examiners. Once described by General Eisenhower as 'the greatest living expert on security', Pinto was a Dutchman who began his intelligence career working for the French Secret Service (the Deuxième Bureau) during the First World War, after which he came to live in England, joining MI5 at the beginning of World War Two. During Pinto's time here, the staff of examiners increased from five to thirty-two.

In October 1942, Pinto transferred to the Dutch Counter-Intelligence Headquarters in London. Following his departure, the 'school' underwent extensive reorganisation and became known as the London Reception Centre, or LRC, although its purpose remained the same. During the latter stages of the war the LRC was gradually wound down, with the staff finally being disbanded on 31 May 1945 having made a considerable contribution to the war effort. Of the 33,000 foreign nationals estimated to have passed through this centralised screening bottleneck, only three enemy agents are known to have avoided detection.

One of the unlucky spies caught here was Alphonse Timmerman and his case, written about in Pinto's autobiographical 'Spycatcher' accounts, offers an insight into this phase of the building's history.

The Timmerman Spy Case

Alphonse Louis Eugène Timmerman, a thirty-seven-year-old Belgian merchant seaman was sent to the LRC for examination in April 1942, after arriving at Glasgow on board a ship. As usual, he was asked to give a preliminary statement before any detailed interrogation began. Next, all of his luggage and personal belongings were minutely inspected in what was known as 'the lumber room', a large room with no furniture apart from a long bare table and some chairs. In here, wrote Pinto, each morning examiners inspected 'the suitcases, briefcases, wallets, pocketbooks, correspondence, fountain-pens, spectacle cases, tobacco pouches, cigarette cases, bunches of keys and all the other paraphernalia carried by the refugees' with the utmost care, using powerful magnifying glasses to examine the tiniest details. The scene, Pinto records, 'used to look like a cross between a customs examination and the vicarage jumble sale.'

Among Timmerman's possessions were a few orange sticks of the type used by ladies to push back the cuticle around their fingernails, a wad of cotton wool and a small envelope containing pyramidon powder. Although each item seemed quite innocent on its own, Pinto was expert enough to know that together they comprised the three essentials for writing in invisible ink: the powder was to be dissolved in a water/alcohol mixture and the cotton wool wrapped around the point of a stick to make a useable writing implement.

Only now did the questioning proper begin, and Timmerman was tricked into admitting that all three of the above items belonged to him. Realising too late that his examiners understood their significance, he broke down and admitted to being a spy working for the Nazis. He was hanged at Wandsworth Prison at nine o'clock in the morning on 7 July 1942.

Wartime Rumours

With activities at the London Reception Centre cloaked in official secrecy, it was inevitable that rumours would circulate about what was 'really' going on behind these forbidding neo-Gothic walls. Some of these stories may yet prove to be true; accurate or not, they are still being repeated today.

One rumour is that a tunnel once linked this building with the nearby prison. Allegedly, this tunnel was used to secretly convey prisoners of war between the two establishments and it has been said that the tunnel was finally filled in during the 1970s. Mark Justin, however, is convinced that no such tunnel ever existed. He is the proprietor of *Le Gothique*, the restaurant and bar that today occupies part of the ground floor of the Royal Victoria Patriotic Building, and he maintains that this rumour was deliberately started by LRC staff following an outcry from well-to-do local residents who feared that Nazis might escape to rape or kill them in their beds. To counter such fears, he believes, a 'secret' story was allowed to leak out that the more dangerous inmates were transported to the prison below ground and thus had no chance whatsoever of slipping away from their captors.

Another story revolves around one of the oddest incidents of the whole of the Second World War: Rudolf Hess's puzzling flight to Britain. Hess was Adolf Hitler's deputy as leader of the Nazi Party but in the spring of 1941 he sensationally decided to enter Britain on a self-appointed mission to negotiate peace between this country and the Third Reich.

On 10 May of that year, he flew in secret from Augsburg and parachuted into Scotland only to be quickly arrested in circumstances that remain shrouded in mystery. His proposal – a promise to respect the integrity of the British Empire so long as the British did not oppose German actions in Europe – was ignored by the British government, who treated him as a prisoner of war and incarcerated him throughout the remainder of the conflict. At the Nuremberg war crimes trials, Hess was sentenced to life imprisonment, serving his sentence at Spandau prison in Berlin until his death in 1987.

Quite why Hess should have chosen the course of action he did remains unsolved. One relatively sober version of events is that by early 1941 his influence within the Nazi Party was waning and that by securing peace with Britain he hoped to score a major personal political victory. Others say that Hess was tricked into coming to Britain in a plot masterminded by British Intelligence. Still others believe that this high-ranking Nazi had secretly arranged peace talks with members of the British Royal Family and that even today the potential for scandal remains so great that official confirmation of this story would damage the monarchy, perhaps irrevocably. And so on… Numerous books have been written concentrating solely on the mystery of Hess's flight to Britain but what is relevant here is the rumour that Hess was interrogated and spent at least part of his time as a prisoner in Wandsworth, confined in the depths of the Royal Victoria Patriotic School.

The most notorious rumours relating to this building, however, are those that talk of torture and execution. It should be stated at the outset that official records maintain that conditions at the 'special school'/London Reception Centre were far from barbaric. According to the Public Records Office, the accommodation provided to inmates was basic but comfortable. They were issued with cigarettes and a small sum of money; they could make use of a football pitch and a croquet lawn; and they were even provided with entertainment in the form of cinema shows and dance bands. Interviews with examiners were relaxed, informal, and usually conducted on a one-to-one basis, and the general feeling among the examiners was that there was simply no need to be heavy-handed. After all, they reasoned, a good ninety-five percent of refugees were completely honest and many had already gone through hell to escape to Britain. And there were practical reasons too: experience showed that interviews were more likely to yield useful information if held in a friendly atmosphere. If a refugee turned out to be an enemy agent, or at least raised strong suspicions, then that individual would be transferred to the sinister 'Camp 020' (at Latchmere House in Ham) for deeper investigation, but in the meantime a tougher form of interrogation was deemed unnecessary.

In his autobiographical accounts, Pinto goes out of his way to stress the humane manner in which people were treated at the 'special school'. For example, he writes: 'As I have mentioned before even the slightest suspicion of physical torture or the inflicting of discomfort on a suspect is not only personally repugnant to me, as it is to any civilised person, but is also firmly disallowed by British law.'

Yet despite such assurances, darker stories of what went on here stubbornly refuse to die, causing some to wonder: does Pinto 'protest too much'? There are claims that suspected spies were imprisoned for years in underground cells, and in windowless concrete chambers specially constructed in the south courtyard, and that examiners were quite prepared to torture suspects to elicit the information they wanted. There are also rumours of prisoners being shot in one of the courtyards and later buried under the cobbles. Mark Justin was told that the pond in the south courtyard marks the site of a concrete bunker where six enemy agents were executed; apparently, the only reason this pond was created was that the builders refurbishing the courtyard were unable to smash through the bunker's concrete base so they decided it would be simpler to just build the walls up and fill the structure with water.

One gruesomely amusing anecdote concerns a would-be spy found swimming in Portsmouth Harbour. When picked up, he said that he had jumped from a German ship, swum right across the Channel and now wanted to fight for the Allies. As usual, he was sent to the London Reception Centre for questioning, where his story just did not seem to add up. The details of his journey did not square with any recognised escape route and his claimed swimming prowess seemed, to say the least, quite remarkable. Deeply suspicious, his examiners are said to have escorted him to Wandsworth Bridge where they tested his swimming ability in the most straightforward and cold-blooded way possible, by throwing him into the Thames to see what would happen! He drowned.

After the War

Following the closure of the London Reception Centre, the Royal Victoria Patriotic Building became for a time a teachers' training college. Then, in 1952 it was purchased by the London County Council, following which it was used as a school, first the Honeywell Secondary Mixed School and then Spencer Park Comprehensive School for Boys. By now, though, the building's age was beginning to take its toll. Parts of the structure were becoming unsafe and during the 1970s Spencer Park was forced to move to new premises.

After this, the abandoned building swiftly deteriorated. The Inner London Education Authority lacked the budget for maintenance, vandals smashed the windows, thieves stole lead from the roofs and water tanks, dry rot damaged much of the woodwork, and thousands of pigeons settled inside. The building was nearly pulled down but following pressure from the Victorian Society and the Wandsworth Society it was granted a Grade II listed status. In the early 1980s, surveyors for Wandsworth Council estimated that restoration would cost approximately £4 million and advised that the most economical course of action would be to convert the derelict structure into a bird sanctuary.

Thankfully, this wonderful old building was saved by businessman Paul Tutton, and today it houses a mixed community of luxury flats, workshops, studios, a bar and restaurant (*Le Gothique*), and a drama school (the Academy of Live and Recorded Arts, or ALRA). Yet despite the successful and welcome conversion the building's extraordinary history maintains a pervasive presence here and there are many stories of uncanny experiences within the old orphanage's walls.

Ghost of the Royal Victoria Patriotic Building

The most famous ghost story concerns the apparition of a young orphan girl from the time of the building's first incarnation and this is said to be the spirit of Charlotte Jane Bennett, who perished in a fire in January 1862. Charlotte was in the second of two days' solitary confinement when she died, locked in the superintendent's bathroom for the terrible crime of 'insubordination'. The tragedy is that her agonised screams were heard but went unanswered by her fellow orphans who were scared to intervene for fear that they too might be punished.

The building's website (www.rvpb.com) carries a variation of this story, stating that the orphanage almost closed down as a result of a scandal 'involving physical and sexual abuse by the rector and the death of one of the orphans'. Charlotte's ghost has been held responsible for numerous weird happenings here. She is said to roam the cloisters of the north and south courtyards where strange noises have been put down to her work, and there is a legend that a ghostly figure can be seen each year on the anniversary of her death, reading a book under a tree in one of the courtyards.

In August 1987, Mark Justin encountered an apparition in a cellar beneath *Le Gothique*. The original cellar doorways were arched and Mark was with a carpenter who was fitting square doors and frames when they were joined by a young girl who stood in the doorway and appeared to listen to the two men as they chatted to her: '... and we are having an entire conversation, one way because there was no reply, to a girl in Edwardian nightdress, asking her how was school and suchlike. We thought that because there's a professional acting school that operates from this building we were talking to one of the students from ALRA – the Academy of Live and Recorded Arts – who was just about to go on stage, or that it was a dress rehearsal. I thought nothing of it. She was just there.'

At lunchtime, the two men came up to the bar and mentioned to others that they had seen a young girl down in the cellar in what appeared to be a costume, and they asked if ALRA was putting on a play that day. It was only when they remembered that the academy had broken for the summer holiday and would not be back for another few weeks that Mark realised the girl could not have been an actor after all. With that realisation, the carpenter – a burly, tattooed individual who did not seem at all the type of person to let himself get spooked – refused to go back down to the cellar and promptly left the building, abandoning all his tools. 'Next thing I hear,' recalled Mark, 'he's on the phone, saying: "Can you put all my saws, tools, chisels in a cab, send it out – I'm not coming back down there"!'

Friday 17 May 1991 was the night before the FA Cup Final between Tottenham Hotspur and Nottingham Forest, and Mark was enjoying a late night drink with nine of his friends, looking forward to their trip to Wembley the next day. As it was a private party all of the doors were closed and locked, and yet something seemed to enter the bar area where they were all sitting at the sofas in one corner. One by one, each man's face took on a puzzled expression as an eerie sensation, coupled with a distinct aroma, brushed against each of them in turn, moving in a circle around the group. 'It was, I think, best described as if someone had a wet salmon and just brushed it across all of our thighs,' says Mark.

Above: *Plaque on the wall of the Royal Victoria Patriotic Building. (James Clark)*

Right: *The north courtyard. (James Clark)*

Nervously, he joked that it was only the resident ghost, before getting up and opening the door to visit the gents' toilet. The next moment, all nine of his friends rushed out through the door, overcome with fear and refusing point blank to return to the bar. Many of the strange happenings in the Royal Victoria Patriotic Building are said to occur at and below ground level, because the upper floors have been substantially rebuilt since the days of the asylum. Nevertheless, a number of odd incidents have been reported from elsewhere in the building and a resident of one of the upper flats told Mark that he occasionally sees a part-apparition walking as if on a floor that no longer exists. 'He's got a mezzanine floor that didn't exist [then],' explained Mark, 'so his experiences are always of some decapitated kind of half figure, which makes sense because the floors in his flat aren't on the right level.'

Philip Hutchinson is an actor who trained at the Academy of Live and Recorded Arts here, and in a talk he gave to The Ghost Club in 2000 he spoke of several strange experiences he and others have had in the building's central tower. (I am grateful to Philip for allowing me to use material from his presentation.) Because the room in which Charlotte Jane Bennett died was located in this tower, incidents here are also usually attributed to her ghost. A technician in the Radio Room (where students have their radio training) was working late one night when the atmosphere suddenly became icy cold. In that same instant, he became convinced he was no longer alone in the room and in the grip of an all-consuming horror – a feeling he had never experienced before – he fled, leaving the room unlocked behind him. It was not until the following morning that he plucked up the courage to return.

The room below the Radio Room was where Philip and his fellow students received singing lessons. One summer day, a friend of Philip's turned up early for a class and found he was the only person there. As the room was hot he decided to open a window. He undid the latches but despite his best efforts to force the window open it stubbornly refused to move. Giving up, he turned around and walked back to his bag to take out what he would need for the lesson. When

Cellar beneath Le Gothique*: in 1987 an apparition was seen in this doorway. (James Clark)*

he looked back, he saw that the previously jammed window was now wide open, swinging freely in a gentle summer breeze.

Philip himself had a somewhat similar experience on the first floor of the tower, outside the room where he was given voice classes. Because he commuted from Hampshire to London every day he needed to catch early trains and as a result was usually one of the first people in the academy each morning. Normally, a caretaker would already have unlocked the classroom door but on this occasion Philip found the door firmly locked and so he settled down to wait, sitting on the steps with his back leaning against the door. After about half an hour his tutor turned up and asked Philip why he was waiting outside. Philip answered that the room was still locked but when the tutor tried the handle it turned without any effort whatsoever and the door swung open.

Further ghostly stories are told of the south courtyard where, Mark Justin informed me, people have reported hearing screams and the sound of voices speaking in German. The pond in this courtyard was allegedly built on the remains of a concrete bunker that, during the dark days of the Second World War, was involved in the clandestine executions of six German spies. The Royal Victoria Patriotic Building is without a doubt one of the most fascinating buildings in London and we can only be grateful that it was saved from its threatened destruction. Readers wishing to take a closer look at this spectacular building can easily do so by visiting the suitably atmospheric *Le Gothique* bar and restaurant, located on the ground floor and accessed via the rear courtyard.

The Haunted Staircase

Not especially well known today, Elliott O'Donnell (1872–1965) was for many years one of Britain's most active ghost-hunters. Descended from an ancient Irish family, a love for the uncanny ran deep in O'Donnell and for half a century he researched and published numerous collections of real-life ghost stories. In his *Haunted Houses of London* (1909) he described the dramatic haunting of a house in Wandsworth.

Royal Victoria Patriotic Building: the central tower.
(James Clark)

Unfortunately, O'Donnell did not know the exact location of the house involved, and could only say that it was a large, old building that lay somewhere close to Wandsworth Common. Moreover, he protected the occupants' identities by giving them fictitious names and so it is impossible to trace the address using historical records. Even so, this must be one of the most bizarre ghost stories ever committed to paper and so it is well worth retelling here.

Stepping into this house, visitors would find themselves in a sizeable entrance hall dominated by a flight of low, broad oak stairs. These led up to a gallery connecting the building's east and west wings. Close inspection of the entrance hall ceiling revealed old marks where the staircase had originally been affixed; it had obviously been moved approximately eight or nine feet (two-and-a-half metres) to one side at some point in the building's history so that it no longer stood quite central, and the result was to make the hall and gallery feel decidedly lop-sided. According to one resident, a 'Mr Scaran', when he first moved in: 'The staircase arrested my attention the moment I entered the house – why, I cannot exactly say, but there was something indefinably odd about it.'

The 'Scaran' Family

A family O'Donnell calls the Scarans rented this house for a while. On their first night, Mr and Mrs Scaran were kept awake by loud creaks and groans from the wooden staircase. It was as if crowds of people were walking up and down the steps. The sounds began at around midnight and continued until two o'clock in the morning when all suddenly fell silent. Of course, it is quite normal to be keenly aware of noises when in unfamiliar surroundings, especially in a large old house settling at night with its timbers and pipes cooling and contracting, but subsequent events would show that something much stranger lay behind these particular sounds.

The following night, Mr Scaran returned home late to find that his wife and family had already retired to bed. The entrance hall was in darkness so he lit a candle and started to climb the stairs but as he placed his foot onto the sixth step he was struck by an icy cold blast of wind. The candle flame went out and at the same moment the staircase collapsed beneath him, sending

Wandsworth Common. (James Clark)

him tumbling to the ground. Lying dazed on the floor, he heard something laugh in the darkness; 'a low, diabolical chuckle, full of satanical glee' was his description.

Staring upwards he was puzzled to see that the marks showing where the staircase had originally joined the ceiling were directly above him. The actual staircase, he now noticed, was several feet away to his left and he could not understand how he had landed so far away. The only explanation that occurred to him seemed impossible: that he seen the hall as it looked in the past and somehow walked several steps up a staircase that was no longer there!

The next family member to have a strange experience was Joan, the eldest daughter. Early one morning she was taking a cup of tea up the apparently empty staircase when she bumped against what felt like the knees of someone sitting on one of the steps. A moment later, the tray was pushed from underneath, and flew out of her hands and over her head, clattering down into the hall below. Something invisible gave a 'short, sharp, ghoulish laugh', sending Joan fleeing in terror to find her brother Dick. When the pair returned a short while later the invisible being had apparently gone.

Until now, Dick had had no direct experience of the weird happenings but that was to change later the same evening. Dick was an athletic young man in the sixth form at his college, and as he jogged up the staircase he was startled to see a young lady walking up a few feet ahead of him. She was dressed in old-fashioned clothing of a type he associated with the period of King Charles II and her black hair was styled in ringlets. Although he could only see her from behind he felt sure she was very beautiful. The lady paused at the top of the stairs, allowing Dick to catch up with her, but before he could introduce himself she turned around to reveal a face so hideous and 'hellish' that Dick stumbled back in horror. Simultaneously, he felt a violent shove that sent him falling backwards into space. Fortunately, the gallery was not especially high and Dick, being fit and agile, was not seriously injured.

It must have seemed to the Scarans that the inexplicable events in the house were becoming ever stranger. A few days later, their youngest daughter, Molly, was alone in the hall as twilight deepened, when she was at once gripped by the uneasy feeling of being stared at. Forcing herself to look around, she could have sworn she saw the staircase move, sliding a little closer to the centre of the entrance hall. As she stared in wonder, it shifted direction and slowly and noiselessly began to glide nearer to her own position, drawing ever closer and closer until it loomed menacingly over the terrified but spellbound girl. The polished wood reflected the dying sunlight and Molly was captivated by the distorted reflections of dozens of faces in the balustrades. At the very last moment, she snapped out of her trance and dodged to one side, just as the bottom step thudded against the wall with a dull boom.

Her hazy recollections of what followed have a nightmarish quality. Every time she made towards a door, the staircase seemed to shift position, cutting off any exit from the darkening hall. Her sense of reality ebbed as a 'thick and suffocating pall' from the staircase wrapped around her; there was 'the whirling and tearing of some monstrous body through the air' and 'an excruciating sensation of being squashed'. She lost consciousness and when she came to, her worried sister Joan was bending over her with a glass of water.

With admirable understatement, Mr Scaran told O'Donnell: 'I began to wonder if it were wise to remain in the house.' Unfortunately, financial constraints meant the family was effectively trapped there. They had taken the house on a three-year lease and could not afford to move to another property and pay two lots of rent. It was fortunate, then, that the next few months brought no further strange happenings, but this happy state of affairs changed when Mr Scaran's nephew, Will, came to visit.

A sailor, the second officer on board an Anglo-Japanese liner, Will had been away from England for over three years and was returning for a spell of rest. He arrived on the second Friday in December to stay with the Scarans for a week to ten days, after which he intended to leave to spend Christmas with his immediate family. Because they knew Will to be thoroughly sceptical regarding ghosts, the Scarans deliberately kept him in the dark about what had been going on. They wanted to see whether he would spontaneously report something and thereby confirm to them they were not going mad. It did not take long. On the Saturday morning, after his very first night in the house, a tired and rather embarrassed Will recounted the fantastic events of the night before.

After everyone else had gone to bed, Will stayed in the study to continue working on a lecture he was due to give to the Geographical Society. He wrote for as long as he could but eventually grew too tired, put away his writing materials, lit a candle and started up the stairs to his bedroom. Before he reached the fourth step he felt – but could not see – somebody knock into him, moving in the opposite direction. He took another step and it happened again, and then a third unseen being cannoned into him. Utterly terrified, Will froze where he was as he realised that the entire staircase, which was now icy cold, was crowded with invisible people. Although their voices were just indistinct whispers he could tell that both men and women were present: he could feel the rich brocade of the ladies' dresses, smell perfume, and hear the tapping of high-heeled shoes, the rattling of swords in scabbards and the sound of men chuckling.

And now he became aware of another, more distant noise: the pounding of a horse's hooves on turf coming from the direction of Wandsworth Common. The pounding grew louder and louder and he began to hear the horse's frantic snorts, and then the hooves were crunching on the gravel around the front gate. Remorselessly, the crunching sound drew closer and closer, and then there was the crash of something large and heavy leaping into the vestibule and smashing open the door. Will knew, without any doubt, that the ghostly horse was now in the apparently empty hall below him: 'I could hear its rider draw in a deep breath and ease himself in the saddle,' he reported. 'I could hear the harness creak beneath his weight, and his spurs jingle.' Then, with a shrill whinny the horse plunged forwards and upwards, ploughing into the invisible crowd upon the stairs.

Will continued: 'Some one – the rider, I presumed – then uttered a few stern words of admonition, which were immediately succeeded by the sound of the swishing of a sword, and a scream – a scream of the most agonizing terror and pain – the pain of a lost limb swallowed up by the terror of a lost soul.' Something Will knew was blood splattered across his face. There was the crack of a pistol shot and more blood showered over him. It seemed then that the horse slipped backwards and crashed over, crushing several members of the invisible crowd beneath it. Other panicked figures pressed invisibly against Will, suffocating him as they stampeded, and as he struggled against their mass he felt the wooden staircase give way beneath them and the entire crowd tumbled to the floor, with Will underneath. His head thudded onto the ground hard and he lost consciousness.

When Will came to he found himself alone and in total darkness. Struggling to his feet he fumbled around for his candle and re-lit it. As its glow illuminated his surroundings he was puzzled to note that the staircase now stood in a different position to earlier. Although he was able to ascend to his bedroom without incident this time, he was, unsurprisingly, unable to sleep at all that night. After this, the phenomena started up again as badly as before. Joan had a similar experience to her sister, when she found herself trapped in the entrance hall where the staircase 'subtly drove her into a corner and tried to choke her'. Molly sprained her ankle after running up what turned out to be a phantom version of the stairs and falling through it to the ground, and Mr Scaran was terrified by the sudden violent snorting of an unseen horse.

The last straw came late one afternoon. Mrs Scaran was walking down the stairs when she suddenly found herself in the midst of a crowd of invisible men who began pushing against her and kissing her. Her screams brought her husband and Dick racing to her aid and they found her in a faint as the phantoms departed with 'loud and mocking laughs'. Despite the heavy financial loss, the Scarans finally decided enough was enough: less than two weeks later – as soon as Mr Scaran had reached an agreement with the landlord – the family left the house forever.

'Mrs Neuville'

In his same book, O'Donnell reports a separate account of a haunted house near Wandsworth Common, this one from a 'Mrs Neuville'. From her description of a certain feature of the building, it seems likely to have been the very same house from which the Scarans fled. Mrs Neuville always had the uncanny feeling that the house's main staircase was somehow alive and watching her. On several occasions she felt certain that it moved 'noiselessly and stealthily' while her attention was elsewhere, snapping back into its correct position the instant she turned around. Certain bends and particular steps filled her with dread as she became convinced 'they harboured some strangely hideous creature', and she grew ever more afraid, her fear increasing each day as the sun set.

Around eight o'clock one August evening, Mrs Neuville was sitting alone in the study when she heard her aunt call from one of the bedrooms above. The rest of the family being out, she dared not keep her aunt waiting for the old lady was notoriously bad-tempered. On the other hand, going to see what she wanted would mean braving the staircase, where evening shadows were already wrapping around the woodwork.

Her aunt's second call roused her from her indecision. She hurried out of the study and began to climb the stairs as quickly as she was able, keeping her gaze fixed downward. But as she ascended she noticed a strange bluish glow on the silver buckles of her shoes and when she glanced up to see what was responsible she was confronted with a truly hideous sight. On the landing directly in front of her, hovering some six feet (1.8 metres) above the floor was a ball of 'cerulean' blue light, which suddenly resolved itself into a ghastly, disembodied head. Utterly petrified, Mrs Neuville could not look away from the hellish thing that hung in the air before her.

'It was big, round and gross,' she told O'Donnell, 'and crowned with a mass of matted, tow-coloured hair. The face, of a sickly yellowish-white, was broader than that of any human being, the features being large in proportion [...] the mouth had long, thin lips, which were wreathed in a fiendish grin. There was no hair on the lower part of the face, and only an inch or two of neck. The leering, mocking eyes were green, and full of malignant expression – an expression that was positively satanic in its intensity.'

At once, the spell was broken as Mrs Neuville's aunt came out onto the landing, furiously shouting for her niece. The hideous apparition vanished instantly and she never saw it again.

Explanations

Mrs Neuville believed that what she had seen was somehow associated with the ground on which the house stood. The Scarans, meanwhile, speculated that the haunting's origins lay in a tragedy that had been played out here many years earlier, in the time of King Charles II (1660–85). Mr Scaran told O'Donnell he had discovered a tradition of a lady who had poisoned her husband on this site and who was herself killed by her victim's twin brother the evening before she was to marry her accomplice. The brother rode his horse into the hall but, after taking his revenge, was attacked by the onlookers and fatally shot, his corpse later being flung into the same grave as his brother. Soon after these deaths, according to the story Mr Scaran recited, it became known that anybody who tried to live in the house quickly left.

Elliott O'Donnell's own conclusion was that more than one force was at work. In the case of the Scaran family, he felt that at least some of the phenomena could be ascribed to 'phantasms of the dead' but he believed that an 'elemental' spirit was also involved, and that the apparently moving staircase was actually this occult entity in disguise, with the real staircase having remained stationary all the time. As for the identity of the hellish head, O'Donnell again suspected the antics of an elemental.

As to why this elemental might have been drawn here, O'Donnell offered various thoughts: perhaps it had been attracted by a former occupant's crime or bestial nature; the ground beneath the house might contain prehistoric relics; or the building itself might have attracted the spirit, either because of its relative isolation or because of its design. In the end though, O'Donnell could only say that the underlying cause remained 'unknown'.

A Ghostly Old Lady

Also in *Haunted Houses of London*, Elliott O'Donnell gives a short account of yet another ghostly encounter in a house in Wandsworth. Thankfully, this one was of a much gentler nature. A lady living here was constantly disturbed by the sound of an old woman talking outside her bedroom door. So often did she hear the sound that the lady grew thoroughly accustomed to it and was not in the least bit afraid of her resident phantom. In fact, she would occasionally call out to the ghost telling it to be quiet, and sometimes the ghost even obeyed! The old woman also appeared frequently as an apparition and was seen by both the lady and her sister in various areas of the house.

As with the events previously described, O'Donnell could not give the house's exact location and it may well have been a completely different building to that in the stories just related. However, one small detail hints that it may have been the same house. This harmless apparition was most often seen gliding along the passages or … on the staircase.

Another Haunted House Near Wandsworth Common?

Another report of a haunted house near Wandsworth Common appeared in the *Wandsworth & Battersea District Times* of 30 December 1899. The exact location of the house involved was withheld and so this report may refer to the same property as featured in the 'The Haunted Staircase'. Then again, perhaps this is yet another ghost story from Wandsworth Borough. The only detail given to identify the house in question was that in May 1887 it was in use as a livery stables.

The family living here – a husband, wife and one child – was allegedly driven out by 'fearful noises' that prevented them from sleeping at night. In one room, the problem was even worse: bedclothes would be pulled onto the floor and then 'would rear up again on to the bed'.

Relatives of the family who stayed overnight in this particular room also found themselves persecuted by mysterious forces. Some unseen being grabbed the husband's sister-in-law by her shoulders and shook her roughly from side to side. When her husband reached out to help her, he cried out in pain as a powerful shock – 'as it were, of electricity' – shot up his arm.

The newspaper reported that after this family's departure, five further families attempted to live here but every one moved out again as soon as they could. In closing, the article stated that the house was henceforth to be left 'permanently untenanted'.

The Grey Lady of Wandsworth Prison

The grim Victorian edifice of HMP Wandsworth apparently has one resident more than the official figures suggest, a gloomily attired female apparition known variously as 'The Grey Lady' and 'Wandsworth Annie'. Over the years, according to an article in the *Wandsworth Borough News* on 23 December 1976, her sad figure has been sighted 'by prisoners and officers alike', drifting through the corridors without a sound.

Sited in Heathfield Road, the prison was originally built as the Surrey House of Correction. Construction began in 1849 and the building began taking in prisoners in 1851, starting in November with exclusively male inmates but admitting female prisoners as well from April 1852. (The female section of the prison was closed some three decades later.) Over the years, its cells have provided unwelcome homes for many infamous inmates, amongst them the notorious East End gangsters the Krays, Great Train Robber Ronald Biggs (who escaped in July 1965) and the 'Acid Bath Murderer' John George Haigh, who was hanged here on 10 August 1949.

Haigh was far from the only person executed at Wandsworth. In total, 135 people were dispatched on the gallows here, among them murderers, traitors and spies. The first was Thomas Smithers, 'The Battersea Murderer', who was hanged on 8 October 1878. The last, another murderer, was Hendryk Niemasz, executed on 8 September 1961 but it was not until 1993 that Wandsworth's gallows – the last remaining in a British prison – was finally dismantled.

Concerning the origin of 'Wandsworth Annie', there are a number of different stories. In one, she is the ghost of a woman who worked as a cook in the prison and died in the 1870s. More usually, however, she is said to be the ghost of a female prisoner. Details are generally vague, although the *Wandsworth Borough News* article referred to above stated that 'Annie is believed to be the ghost of a middle-aged woman who had died in the prison some 20 years after it was opened as a house of correction for men and women'. Descriptions of the apparition as a veiled figure wearing shabby grey clothing do accord with the theory that she was a prisoner and not a cook, as a female prisoner at Wandsworth at this time would have been made to wear a dark veil to conceal her identity. As to the identity of that prisoner, some say the ghost is that of a suicide, but many others maintain that the Grey Lady is most likely the spectral shade of one Kate Webster, the second person and only woman to be executed on the gallows here.

Kate Webster

Kate, or Catherine, Webster was born in County Wexford in Ireland, and was involved in petty crime for most of her life. In January 1879, the thirty-year-old Kate might have made a new

HMP Wandsworth. (James Clark)

HMP Wandsworth: the main gate.
(Stewart McLaughlin)

Veiled female prisoner at HMP Wandsworth in the 1850s:
the outfit matches descriptions of the apparition seen here.
(Stewart McLaughlin)

start for herself when she entered the service of Mrs Julia Thomas, a comfortably well-off lady living at No. 2 Vine Cottages (later No. 9 Park Road) in Richmond. Very quickly, however, the shoddiness of Kate's work and her fondness for a drink irritated her employer and after receiving a number of reprimands Kate was given notice to leave.

Throughout February, tensions in the house increased as Kate resentfully worked out her notice and Mrs Thomas became increasingly frightened of her servant. On Sunday 2 March, events came to a tragic conclusion. Mrs Thomas had been to church and Kate had been drinking in a local pub called the Hole in the Wall, and when Mrs Thomas arrived home that evening a violent row erupted between the two women. 'In the height of my anger,' Kate later stated, 'I threw her from the top of the stairs to the ground floor.'

The precise details of what happened to cause Mrs Thomas's death are unclear, but it was what happened after her demise that ensured her killer's notoriety. Dragging the older woman's body into the kitchen, Kate proceeded to saw the corpse into pieces, which she later boiled or burned. Most of the grisly remains she then packed into a large wooden box but the head, which would not fit, she placed inside a black bag.

Wearing one of Mrs Thomas's fine dresses, Kate travelled to Hammersmith to visit her friends, the Porter family. She took the black bag with her but during her visit she slipped away from the Porters' for a short time and when she returned the bag had vanished. That night, Kate disposed of the rest of the body, unwittingly aided by the Porters' son, Robert. Carrying the heavy box between them across Richmond Bridge, Kate informed the young lad that she was meeting someone who would collect the box from her and told him to go on without her. As he walked ahead, Robert heard a loud splash from behind him, and a few moments later Kate rejoined him.

The box and its gruesome contents were quickly discovered but without the head it was not possible for police to identify the remains and, as the real Mrs Thomas had not yet been reported as missing, the find was reported in the papers as 'The Barnes Mystery'. In mid-March, however, the sight of furniture from Vine Cottage being readied for sale aroused a neighbour's suspicions; the alarm was raised and police began to search for Kate Webster in connection with the murder of Mrs Thomas and the theft of her property.

Kate fled to Ireland but she was swiftly arrested and brought back to England to be tried at the Old Bailey, a trial marked by numerous lies and inconsistencies in her testimony. One especially macabre detail that came out was the Hole in the Wall landlady's statement that a day or two after the murder Kate Webster visited the pub and offered to sell her jars of what she said was dripping but which was probably the fatty residue from boiling Mrs Thomas's flesh. The jury found Kate guilty of murder and she was sentenced to death.

Sitting in her cell at Wandsworth Prison, the condemned Kate gradually became resigned to her fate and on 28 July she admitted to the murder in a detailed statement to her solicitor, Mr O'Brien. Later the same day, she made a full confession to the Roman Catholic priest attending her. That evening, the hangman William Marwood readied the gallows that would take her life.

On the morning of Tuesday 29 July 1879, C.J. Colville (under-sheriff of Surrey), Dr Wynter (surgeon) and Captain Colville (the prison governor) gathered at Wandsworth Prison's execution shed to await her arrival. As recorded in the *Illustrated Police News* of 2 August 1879: 'Just before nine the procession started for the scaffold, Father McEnnery reading the burial service. The prison bell commenced tolling at a quarter to nine, and at three minutes past that hour the black flag was hoisted on the flagpole, denoting that Catherine Webster was no more. The appearance of the flag was greeted with some cheering by the crowd.' The *Illustrated Police News* account quoted above stated that Catherine Webster was no more. Those who have witnessed HMP Wandsworth's Grey Lady may beg to differ.

Chapter Six

ACROSS WANDSWORTH BOROUGH

The Kingston Zodiac

The 1970s saw the publication of Mary Caine's *The Kingston Zodiac*, a book purporting to reveal the truth about the landscape around Kingston-upon-Thames in Surrey. Caine believed that a set of ancient, magical images was outlined in the roads, paths and rivers surrounding Kingston, and the images she described were so large that her Zodiac encompasses parts of Wandsworth Borough. Her book was not the first such attempt to divine mystical meaning from the English landscape. In 1935, an artist named Katharine Maltwood claimed to have discovered (or rediscovered) a group of enormous images drawn in the natural features surrounding Glastonbury in Somerset. Because of their correspondence with the constellations, Maltwood referred to the group as 'The Temple of the Stars', and she believed this was the original round table of Arthurian legend.

Caine was spurred into a similar study looking at Kingston's surroundings after a friend commented how many of her local pubs had Zodiacal names such as The Ram and The Bull. Drawing a circle around Kingston approximately twelve miles (nineteen kilometres) in diameter, she studied maps and delved into legends, and images started to reveal themselves to her. First, she identified the representation of a lion, then she spotted the image of a pair of twins, and others gradually followed.

In all, she discovered thirteen images: the twelve signs of the Zodiac and the additional figure of a huge hound standing guard over the circle. Within each figure she interpreted place names, legends and historical events as revealing the astrological influences governing a particular area. Whitton and Hounslow, for example, lay under the influence of Aries, which in turn is ruled by Mars, the god of war, underlining these areas' many militaristic associations. Kingston itself is governed by Libra, the sign of justice, which Caine felt might explain why Surrey's county law courts were sited there. As for Wandsworth, two Zodiacal signs fall across lands within this borough's borders.

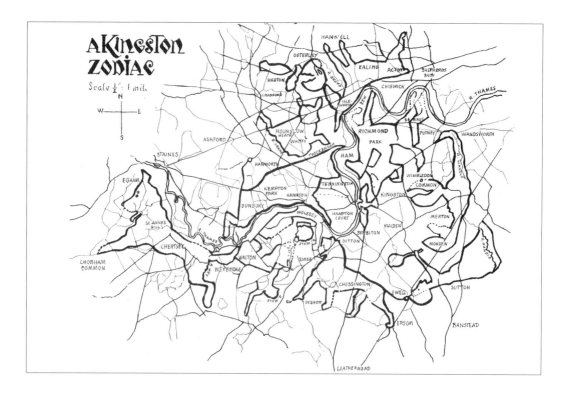

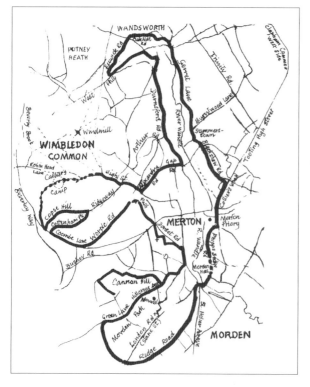

Above: *Mary Caine's drawing of the Kingston Zodiac. (Mary Caine)*

Left: *Scorpio, the Zodiac's death sign, by Mary Caine. (Mary Caine)*

Opposite: *Burntwood Lane meets Garratt Lane, the point at which Caine's two interpretations of Scorpio's tail diverge: appropriately, the building on this corner is currently home to 'Co-operative Funeralcare'! (James Clark)*

Scorpio

The first of these signs is Scorpio. Caine described this as the Zodiac's death sign, and saw one effect of this rather gloomy astrological influence in the many burial places falling within its boundaries. Scorpio's outline is traced in Caine's drawing. Although Wandsworth has not been caught by the scorpion's claws (which lie very roughly across Morden Park and Wimbledon), the borough does not escape its deadly sting. Exactly how the tail and sting should be depicted, though, left Caine in two minds. Her first suggestion was that this part of the scorpion follows the River Wandle as far north as Wandsworth High Street and then curves westward along West Hill. On the other hand, she thought, it might continue northeast through Upper Tooting, drawn by lines begun with Burntwood Lane and Tooting High Street before curving northwards along Clapham Common West Side.

In the Glastonbury Zodiac, the 'eastern water-gate' is guarded by the relatively unusual arrangement of two churches standing opposite each other across a river. Likewise, the eastern point at which the Thames enters the Kingston Zodiac sees the churches of Fulham and Putney facing each other across the water (see 'The Church That Giants Built', page 48). It is here that Scorpio meets the second of the borough's signs, Sagittarius.

Sagittarius

Often depicted as a centaur, Sagittarius appears here as an archer mounted on horseback. His sign hangs upside down with the Thames looping around to make room for his steed's legs. The horse's rear and tail just about fall across Wandsworth Borough's western edge. It is not clear whether the archer is helmeted or hooded, and in this ambiguity he recalls myths of both King

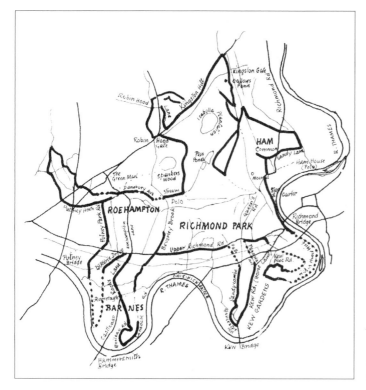

Sagittarius, by Mary Caine.
(Mary Caine)

Arthur and Robin Hood. To Caine, both of these characters were essentially representations of the sun king who fights for justice and dies for his people.

Robin Hood was of course an outlaw, and Caine remarked how a number of highwaymen operated within the bounds of her Sagittarius figure. The highwayman sign hanging at Tibbet's Corner (see 'The Highwayman Who Never Existed', page 55) is 'whisked by the horse's tail', for example, and she suggested a correspondence between the nearby Green Man pub at Putney Heath, once a favourite watering hole for highwaymen (see 'Putney's Haunted Heath', page 50), and Sherwood Forest's famous hooded man clad in Lincoln Green.

Another theme that recurs throughout this figure is the horse and Caine noted numerous examples of places and buildings that are in one way or another linked to this animal. These include Ye Olde Spotted Horse pub in Putney High Street and the (since closed) Maltese Cat pub in Aubyn Square, Roehampton, the latter named after a polo pony in a story by Kipling.

The 'thumb-print of the Creator'

The thirteen huge images within the Kingston Zodiac are shaped primarily by natural features, although human handiwork too plays a part in completing the outlines. Comparisons of Caine's drawings with old maps show that many of her lines follow ancient roads and rivers, thus needing only a minimal leap of faith to believe that the revealed influences are an intrinsic aspect of the landscape. But critics would point out that some of the features she uses were actually shaped relatively recently.

Such objections can be countered by Caine's suggestion that where human beings have helped to define the images it is because profound cosmic forces can affect our actions, even if we are unaware of it. Thus, new roads and developments may continually change the details of the landscape but the Kingston Zodiac – its magical pattern imprinted upon the very essence of our planet – will always emerge, revealing itself to those with eyes to see. It is, in Caine's words, the 'thumb-print of the Creator'.

This short description can only touch upon the rich poeticism of Caine's visionary landscape interpretations, but her original book has since been revised and republished by Capall Bann Publishing, and the new edition is easily available to those who wish to learn more.

Spring-heeled Jack: The Leaping Terror

During the first half of the nineteenth century much of what is now Greater London consisted of rural villages scattered around the London metropolis. As the young Queen Victoria, then a graceful and silver-voiced eighteen-year-old, was settling into the first year of her reign, those villages began to be troubled by some very dark rumours. Something evil was haunting the night, and it was attacking people.

In September 1837, that something – apparently a 'ghost, imp or devil' in the shape of 'a large white bull' – carried out a number of assaults in Barnes, mostly on women. As a result, according to *The Morning Chronicle* of 10 January 1838, 'no respectable female [had] since left home after dark without a male companion'. Fear spread swiftly and similar stories were soon circulating among other villages to the west and south of London. Some people blamed the attacks on a band of cruel young aristocrats who were supposedly dressing up and frightening people to win a bet, but many others were convinced that a genuine demon was wandering abroad.

Early descriptions of this mysterious figure vary considerably, which must have added to the confusion and fear. Whereas some witnesses described a large white animal (typically a bear or a bull), others talked of a ghost, a figure in full shining armour (somewhat like the apparition of Hamlet's father), a black-cloaked fiend or even the Devil himself. Was this demon able to change his form? Or might there be more than one?

As days and nights passed, the stories developed. It was said that people had had their clothes and flesh torn by monstrous iron claws and that several women had been scared quite literally to their deaths. Many of the reported attacks seemed to follow a pattern: the assailant would leap from the shadows without warning, commit his crime and then bound away back into the darkness. Those leaps, people said, were unnatural. No mortal man could jump that far or that high. Such claims fuelled speculation as to the attacker's supernatural origin.

More sceptical folk were unwilling to believe such nonsense and asserted that the attacker must be a man wearing boots soled with India-rubber, or that there was some sort of spring-loaded mechanism in the boots' heels, although they hesitated to provide details as to how such a device might work in practice. As the stories grew increasingly lurid, attacks were reported more frequently and from an ever-widening area. For a time, just about any unsolved incident was automatically declared to be the work of this mysterious assailant. He, or it, was referred to by any of several names, including 'the Suburban Ghost' and 'the Leaping Terror', but by February 1838 the newspapers were using the name we remember today: Spring-heeled Jack.

With his name now agreed upon, descriptions of Jack's appearance started to become more standardised. Jack was male, tall and thin, with a gaunt face and eyes that glowed like red balls of fire. He wore a voluminous black cloak and some sort of headgear, often described as a helmet.

'Pig Hill Path'/Latchmere Road. (James Clark)

Blue and white fire crackled around his open mouth and, it was said, he would vomit these flames directly into his victim's face. As for his hands, these were cold and hard, like claws. He was described in *The Times* of 22 February 1838 as 'hideous and frightful' to behold.

Spring-heeled Jack in Battersea

The lonely roads and lanes around London were dangerous to travel alone in the 1830s, especially after dark, but a young woman named Mary Stevens had been visiting relatives on the edge of the Battersea Marshes and was making her way back to Lavender Hill where she was in service at one of the large houses. The story of what happened on her journey is recounted in *Stand and Deliver* by Elizabeth Villiers (1928).

It was a miserable night. Rain was drizzling and it was growing late, and so Mary decided to take a shortcut, climbing up the steep Pig Hill Path towards the crown of Lavender Hill. ('Pig Hill Path', as it is marked on the 1838 tithe map of Battersea, corresponds to the modern Latchmere Road.) At that time, the area had a rural feel to it and somewhere around here was the opening of 'a narrow, rather winding passage' leading from Lavender Hill to Clapham Common, that was the object of superstitious dread. According to Villiers, this lonely passage had the gruesome nickname of 'Cut-throat Lane' (not to be confused with the 'Cutthroat Lane' mentioned in 'Putney's Haunted Heath', page 50) and stories were told of footpads slitting the throats of travellers and taking their gold, and of a jealous lover who lured his unfaithful sweetheart into the lane to kill her and then committed suicide over her lifeless body.

Unsurprisingly, Mary felt nervous as she emerged onto Lavender Hill and she began to run, her steps clattering ever faster as she neared the opening of that narrow lane. Beyond the turnstile barring its mouth, the way was hidden in impenetrable blackness. Mary was just drawing level with it when a tall figure leaped out from the shadows, clearing the stile 'with a single bound'. Before she could react, the figure reached her side, took her roughly in his arms, gripped her firmly and kissed her. Then he released his hold with a loud laugh and 'leaping extraordinarily high, vanished into the night as mysteriously as he had come.'

Lavender Hill, looking west towards The Falcon. (James Clark)

Reading this from the comfort of an armchair, there is something vaguely comical about this brief episode and we can almost picture Jack here as the dastardly villain of an old melodrama, twirling his moustache as he bounds away into the shadows. But to Mary Stevens, alone in the cold darkness of that rainy night, the sudden attack was utterly terrifying and she collapsed to the ground screaming in horror.

A group of men at the Falcon inn a short distance down the hill came out to see what was happening and discovered Mary in hysterics. Despite searching they found no trace of the man who had assaulted her and so they took Mary to her master's house, where they gathered in the kitchen to hear her strange story. Clearly something had happened to her but the tale she told seemed incredible. It was, they decided, quite possible that some prankster had jumped out at her as she passed by and had stolen a kiss, but surely the description of her attacker was the exaggerated recollection of a hysterical young woman. Yet the following night, just a few miles away, there was another bizarre incident.

It happened a short distance outside the modern-day boundary of Wandsworth Borough, in Streatham High Road, and once again the source for this report is Villiers. As a carriage was rattling its way home from London, the horses were startled by something leaping across the road. The animals bolted and the carriage crashed, badly injuring both the coachman and footman. Although the former did not see what happened, the footman reported that some sort of huge creature, 'whether man or bird or beast he could not say' had bounded from the shadows on one side of the road and leaped clean across to the other side, where it vanished over the top of a high wall. After this incident, increasing numbers of encounters were reported until it seemed that 'everyone who lived near the range of commons – Clapham, Wandsworth, Tooting and Streatham – had some strange tale to tell'.

Although, frustratingly, Villiers does not give dates for any of these sightings and I have been unable to track down any further information, this comment implies that these reports were made during the height of the Spring-heeled Jack 'flap': that is, during the early months of 1838.

Spring-heeled Jack leaps from the shadows, terrifying Mary Stevens. (Anthony Wallis: www.ant-wallis-illustration.co.uk)

*The Falcon, near Clapham
Junction station. (James Clark)*

An Encounter on Tooting Bec Common

Villiers also gives details of another encounter with Spring-heeled Jack, this time on Tooting Bec
Common. She claims to have heard this tale from the eyewitness herself, whom she describes
as being a 'very old lady' (although she emphasised that the lady remained mentally alert with a
clear memory). When she was younger, this lady lived in a house on Tooting Bec Common, not
very far from a stream beside which was a gipsy camp. Most of the people who lived around the
common were suspicious of the gipsies but she was sympathetic towards them, so much so that
when fever broke out in their camp, she risked infection to bring them food and medicine. Her
kindness earned her their lasting gratitude and she recalled how she once lost a brooch on the
common and the gipsies searched for hours until they found it in the grass and returned it.

On one of her visits to the camp, she came out from the tent of an especially ill woman to
find that evening was closing in and mist had shrouded the common. She and her maid promptly
set off for home, accompanied by six or so of the gipsy men, who offered to escort them safely
back. The camp was a good distance behind them and they were nearing their destination when,
suddenly, Jack appeared:

> Out of the mist he leaped, making straight toward the two women with bounds so wide and
> high his identity was unmistakable. In answer to her scream the gipsy guard came up at the
> double, and seeing them the figure paused midway, then wheeling round went leaping off in
> the other direction.

Quickly recovering from her initial shock, the lady had the presence of mind to stand and
observe the strange figure as he retreated. Despite the mist, she could see him clearly and was
able to give a very interesting description. He wore dark clothing and seemed to have a cloak
wrapped around him, but unlike in many other reports, this Jack did not appear to be particularly
tall, nor did he seem to be wearing any sort of headgear. Furthermore, although he jumped over
'good-sized furze bushes and clumps of gorse with no apparent effort', his agility did not seem to
be quite as preternatural as might have been expected. As Villiers put it: 'He was doing far more

91

Tooting Bec Common (James Clark)

than an ordinary man could have accomplished without mechanical aid, but nothing resembling the exploits with which he was credited by rumour.'

The witness believed that a good horseman could have ridden fast enough to overtake the leaping figure, but she and her companions were on foot and Jack escaped into the mist and gathering gloom. Once again, no date is given for this encounter. The feeling from the text is that it took place during the main Spring-heeled Jack scare in early 1838, yet this seems somewhat unlikely. Villiers's book was published in 1928, and if this incident occurred while the old woman was a young lady it seems more probable that the date was some years after 1838. This is quite possible because, although the main 'flap' of Spring-heeled Jack sightings lasted for only a few months, the legend of this bizarre character never completely died away.

Stories of Spring-heeled Jack attacks were reported from around the country for many decades, with notable sightings in Peckham (1872), Aldershot (1877) and Liverpool (1904). In the late 1870s, Jack struck in Mitcham, just to the south of Wandsworth Borough. (For further information about Spring-heeled Jack in Mitcham, see my *Strange Mitcham*.)

Who, or what, was Jack?

So, who was Spring-heeled Jack? There has been no shortage of theories, many of which are as bizarre as Jack himself. To some, the original attacks were the work of a mad pieman who later committed suicide by jumping into the Thames before he was caught. To others, he was a deformed (hence the red eyes) lunatic escaped from an asylum, or perhaps an insane circus fire-eater-cum-acrobat.

Some believe the original perpetrator was a young Irish nobleman named Henry de la Poer Beresford, the Marquis of Waterford. Even more colourful ideas range from a kangaroo (which had either escaped after being kept illegally as a pet, or which had been dressed up by a mad animal trainer) to the idea put forward in a *Flying Saucer Review* article dated May–June 1961 that Jack was an alien visitor who had arrived in a spaceship.

It is very likely that many of the stories told about Jack were of a type we today call urban legends and that much of what was happening can best be understood in these terms. Such

Rectory Lane, Tooting. (James Clark)

an interpretation is supported by the way the reports spread and the difficulty contemporary investigators had in tracking down first-hand witnesses. Consider, for example, the following comment from the *Morning Herald* of 10 January 1838: '…although the stories were in everybody's mouth, no person who had actually seen the ghost could be found.'

It may also be significant that early Victorian England was a turbulent place. After 1836, an economic depression accompanied by a series of bad harvests had provoked an increase in social conflict. In other words, there was just the right climate of fear and uncertainty for such scare stories to flourish. Nevertheless, a number of the reported attacks were certainly authentic in that there were genuine victims, although how many of these attacks inspired the stories about Jack and how many were inspired by them is impossible to say, for it seems that more than one Spring-heeled Jack was at large. Indeed, several people were captured and brought to trial for impersonating him and doubtless many others went uncaught.

An article from Dickens's weekly *All the Year Round* (9 August 1884) commented that Jack's notoriety 'seems to have had the effect of making many silly young men emulous to enact the ruffian in a small way, considering it the height of cleverness to frighten women and children out of their wits, under the belief that Spring-heeled Jack was attacking them.' I am grateful to Mike Dash for forwarding a copy of this recently rediscovered article to me. At least one of these imitators played his jokes in Tooting, in Back-lane (now Rectory Lane). The following comes from a *Balham, Tooting, Mitcham News & Mercury* article of 20 January 1939, containing reminiscences of life in what were for that author the good old days: 'We had some fun in the old village. A fellow dressed in a sheet used to frighten people as "Spring Heeled Jack" in Back-lane, which was unlighted and lonely.'

Perhaps, though, at the heart of all the exaggerations, impersonations and layers of mythology, there really was an 'original' Spring-heeled Jack who brought a strange kind of terror to early Victorian London and its environs, but if so his identity will forever remain uncertain. One of the few things that can be confidently stated about this curious bogeyman is that the mystery surrounding him will endure.

MAP

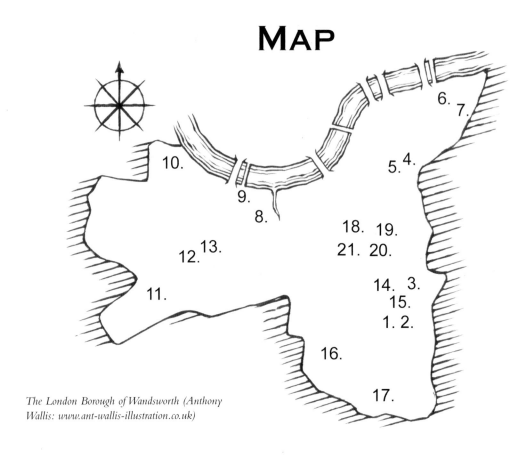

The London Borough of Wandsworth (Anthony
Wallis: www.ant-wallis-illustration.co.uk)

BALHAM
1. The Curious Case of Charles Bravo
2. The Ghost in the Garden
3. Strange Happenings at the Bedford

BATTERSEA
4. Battersea's 'Poltergeist Girl'
5. The 'Mystery House' of Eland Road
6. The Haunting of Battersea Dog and Cats Home
7. Fruit and Veg … and a Ghost

PUTNEY
8. A Putney Poltergeist
9. The Church that Giants Built
10. The White Lady of Ranelagh
11. Putney's Haunted Heath

12. The Highwayman Who Never Existed
13. The Spectral Horse of Colebrook Lodge

TOOTING
14. Thomas Hardy: The Return of the Novelist?
15. The Phantom Smacker of Marius Road
16. 'It Was Like a Horror Movie…'
17. The Tunnel, the Ghost and the 'Resurrection Men'

WANDSWORTH
18. Spooks At The Royal Victoria Patriotic Building
19. The Haunted Staircase
20. Another Haunted House Near Wandsworth Common?
21. The Grey Lady of Wandsworth Prison

SELECT BIBLIOGRAPHY

Borrow, George: *Lavengro*, 1851

Bridges, Yseult: *How Charles Bravo Died: The Chronicle of a Cause Célèbre*, The Reprint Society Ltd, London, 1956

Caine, Mary: *The Kingston Zodiac*, Capall Bann Publishing, 2001 (available from Capall Bann Publishing, Freshfields, Chieveley, Berks. RG20 8TF; website at www.capallbann.co.uk)

Clark, James: *Strange Mitcham,* Shadowtime Publishing, Mitcham, Surrey, 2002 (available by mail order from Shadowtime Publishing, 102 St James Road, Mitcham, Surrey, CR4 2DB; website at www.shadow-timepublishing.co.uk)

Dash, Mike: *'Spring-heeled Jack – to Victorian bugaboo from suburban ghost'*, Fortean Studies Volume 3, London, 1996

Field, John: *Place Names of Greater London*, BT Batsford Ltd, London, 1980

Grose, Francis Grose: *Provincial Glossary With a Collection of Local Proverbs and Popular Superstitions*, London, 1787 (1811 edition)

Haining, Peter: *The Legend and Bizarre Crimes of Spring Heeled Jack*, Frederick Muller, London, 1977

Lambert, S.E: *A History of Tooting: Being a Paper read before the Tooting Ratepayers' Association*, 1884

McLaughlin, Stewart: *Execution Suite: A History of the Gallows at Wandsworth Prison 1878–1993,* HMP Wandsworth, 2004

McLaughlin, Stewart: *Wandsworth Prison: A History,* HMP Wandsworth, 2001

Marryat, Capt. Frederick: *Jacob Faithful*, 1834

Morden, W.E.: *The History of Tooting-Graveney, Surrey: Compiled from original Documents*, Edmund Seale, London, 1897

O'Donnell, Elliott: *Haunted Houses of London*, E. Nash, London, 1909

Pinto, Lt. Col. Oreste: *The Spycatcher Omnibus: The Spy and Counter-Spy Adventures of Lt.-Col. Oreste Pinto*, Hodder and Stoughton Ltd, London, 1962

Public Record Office, edited by Oliver Hoare: *Camp 020: MI5 and the Nazi Spies. The Official History of MI5's Wartime Interrogation Centre*, 2000

Price, Harry: *Poltergeist: Tales of the Supernatural*, Bracken Books, London, 1993 (originally published in 1945 as Poltergeist Over England)

Ruddick, James: *Death at the Priory: Love, Sex and Murder in Victorian England*, Atlantic Books, London, 2001

Taylor, Bernard and Clarke, Kate: *Murder at the Priory: The Mysterious Poisoning of Charles Bravo*, Grafton Books, London, 1988

Underwood, Peter: *Haunted London*, Fontana, 1975

Villiers, Elizabeth: *Stand and Deliver: The Romantic Adventures of Certain Gentleman of the High Toby, Their Times, Their Associates, Friends and Victims,* London, Stanley Paul, London, 1928

Walford, E: *Greater London: A Narrative of its History, its People, and its Places, Volumes I and II*, London, Paris and New York, Cassell & Co. Ltd., 1884

Westwood, Jennifer: *Albion: A Guide to Legendary Britain*, Paladin, London, 1987

Whichelow, Clive: *Local Highwaymen*, Enigma Publishing, London, 2000 (available by mail order from Enigma Publishing, 4 Charnwood Avenue, London SW19 3EJ; website at www.enigmapublishing.co.uk)

Williams, John: *Suddenly at the Priory*, Penguin, London, 1957

Other local titles published by Tempus

Haunted Brighton

ALAN MURDIE

From the ghost who spelt out 'prove me innocent!' at Preston Manor to the skull who screamed in an antique shop in the Lanes, and featuring apparitions, manifestations and first-hand encounters with polite ghosts, malign presences and poltergeists, this collection of stories contains both well-known and hitherto unpublished cases of hauntings from in and around Brighton and is bound to captivate anyone interested in the supernatural history of the area.

0 7524 3829 8

Haunted Hastings

TINA LAKIN

From the haunted staircase at Hastings Library in Claremont and the singing spectre of Hastings College, to the mysterious witches' footsteps in the Stag Inn and the phantom coach and horses that gallops up the High Street on a dark winter's night, *Haunted Hastings* contains a chilling range of new and well-known tales of ghostly goings-on, and will delight both ghost hunters and lovers of ghost stories alike.

0 7524 3827 1

Haunted Kent

JANET CAMERON

Haunted Kent contains spooky stories from around the county, including the hunchback monk of Boughton Malherbe, the black dog of Leeds, and the well-known tale of Lady Blanche of Rochester Castle. This fascinating collection of strange sightings and happenings in the county's streets, churches, public houses and country lanes is sure to appeal to anyone wanting to know why Kent is known as the most haunted county in England.

0 7524 3605 8

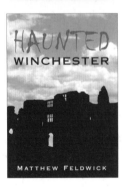

Haunted Winchester

MATTHEW FELDWICK

From tales of spectral monks at Winchester Cathedral and phantom horses in the Cathedral Close to the sad story of Dame Alice Lisle, condemned to death by Judge Jeffreys yet still walking distractedly through the rooms of the Eclipse Inn to this day, this phenomenal gathering is bound to captivate anyone wanting to know the terrifying history of the ghosts and phantoms of historic Winchester.

0 7524 3846 8

If you are interested in purchasing other books published by Tempus, or in case you have difficulty finding any Tempus books in your local bookshop, you can also place orders directly through our website

www.tempus-publishing.com